Gathering Up The Fragments

Preaching As Spiritual Practice

Mariann Edgar Budde

CSS Publishing Company, Inc., Lima, Ohio

GATHERING UP THE FRAGMENTS

Copyright © 2009 by
CSS Publishing Company, Inc.
Lima, Ohio

Scripture quotations are from the New Revised Standard Version of the Bible, copyright 1989 by the Division of Christian Education of the National Council of the Churches of Christ in the USA. Used by permission.

Library of Congress Cataloging-in-Publication Data

Budde, Mariann Edgar, 1959-
   Gathering up the fragments : preaching as spiritual practice / Mariann Edgar Budde.
      p. cm.
   ISBN-13: 978-0-7880-2605-8 (alk. paper)
   ISBN-10: 0-7880-2605-4 (alk. paper)
   1. Church year sermons. 2. Preaching. I. Title.

   BV30.B765 2009
   252'.6—dc22
                                                                    2008035815

For more information about CSS Publishing Company resources, visit our website at www.csspub.com or email us at csr@csspub.com or call (800) 241-4056.

ISBN-13: 978-0-7880-2605-8
ISBN-10: 0-7880-2605-4   PRINTED IN USA

To the people of
St. John's Episcopal Church,
Minneapolis

The self is an inexhaustible supply of sermons.

— Rabbi Edwin Friedman

Table Of Contents

Introduction   7

Preaching As Prayer   13

Building The Foundation, Part One:
   Preaching As We Live And Lead   19

Building The Foundation, Part Two:
   Preaching As Lifelong Study   23

Beginning In Earnest: Letting God Speak
   Through The Texts   29

Paying Attention   33

Who Will Hear What We Preach?   41

Creating Community Out Of A Crowd   51

Public Life And Prophetic Call   59

The Sermon As Art   71

The Gift Of A Sermon   77

A Year Of Sermons
Advent 2   83
   You Are Responsible For Your Rose

Christmas Eve   89
   Living By The Light We Have Known

Epiphany 2/Martin Luther King Sunday   93
   What Shall Become Of The Dreamer's Dream?

Epiphany 6   101
   Where Healing And Acceptance Meet

Ash Wednesday 109
    Forty Days — A Long Time But Not Too Long

Lent 2 115
    You, Too, Can Be Born Again

Lent 3 121
    The Antidote To Anger

Lenten Season 129
    Gathering Up The Fragments

Palm Sunday 135
    A Different Kind Of Power

Easter Day 139
    Trusting The Rope Will Hold

Easter Day 147
    Easter Imperatives

The Ascension Of Our Lord or Memorial Day 153
    Jesus Doesn't Divide The World

The Day Of Pentecost 159
    A Force To Contend With

Proper 12, Pentecost 10, Ordinary Time 17 165
    Confidence In Prayer

Proper 16, Pentecost 14, Ordinary Time 21 171
    How Well Do You Know Him?

Proper 18, Pentecost 16, Ordinary Time 23 or Labor Day 179
    Work And Rest

Proper 24, Pentecost 22, Ordinary Time 29
or Stewardship Sunday 185
    Nothing, Some, Or All

All Saints 193
    Character Is A Lifetime Job

Introduction

I am a minister of a medium-sized congregation, a vocation much like that of a country doctor. Like most parish clergy, I am a generalist with responsibility for the health and well being of an entire congregation. The gift of my work is its comprehensiveness, as I pay attention to all areas of ministry and how they fit together. Life is anything but boring. In a given week, I am in pastoral relationships with several people, I collaboratively plan worship services and preside at them, I teach a class, I work with congregational leaders on future initiatives, and I meet with an elected official on a matter of public concern. I oversee the work of our small, dedicated staff and tend to the task of leadership development throughout the parish. A high school graduate will call to ask for a letter of recommendation for college. A beloved member will be diagnosed with a serious disease. Children will be born and baptized. The roof will leak.

For all the varied tasks of my week, one remains constant. Nearly every Sunday morning I stand before the community and speak of God. I proclaim the good news of Jesus Christ, reflecting on our sacred texts in light of life as we live it and as it comes to us. I preach Christ's death and resurrection as experienced through events in our culture and the larger world, the life challenges and opportunities my parishioners face each day, and the questions of my own heart. Week after week, Sunday morning comes with remarkable and frustrating regularity. While I never know in advance what I will say, I know that I must say something. There is no other option.

In this regard, the preacher's vocation is like that of a farmer with cows to milk each morning, a journalist with a weekly deadline, or even that of a radio show host, as described by Garrison Keillor of National Public Radio's *A Prairie Home Companion*:

> *A weekly radio show keeps a man firmly harnessed in the present. Or, in my case, to Wednesday, Thursday, Friday, and Saturday ... Ask me about 1981 or 1992*

7

and I would have to think hard, but I am intimate with
Thursday afternoon. It's when the rubber meets the
pavement. Friday is when I write scripts. Saturday
morning is when I write the News *from Lake Wobegon.*
Saturday at 5 p.m. we go on the air. By Sunday morn-
ing I've forgotten about that show and am thinking
about the next. In this way, a man avoids melancholy.[1]

Preachers, too, live in the present, last week's sermon forgotten, the next already in mind. We know that the worst time to receive a compliment for last Sunday's sermon is Thursday afternoon, or whenever it is for us that rubber meets pavement, moving this week's sermon to the forefront of our anxiety, if not its actual work. We may have a dozen tasks to attend to before sitting down to write our sermons, but preparing for Sunday mornings is the only one on our minds. The good news is that we can only worry for so long. Deadlines are deadlines.

For on Sunday morning we preach, regardless of what kind of week we've had and how much or little time we've had to prepare. We preach in season and out — how we feel on any given Sunday could not be more irrelevant. We preach through pain and joy, anxiety and confidence, in the soothing, sometimes monotonous rhythms of ordinary time and in the aftermath of disaster. We preach words of judgment and comfort, responsibility and grace. Week after week, we rise with preachers everywhere to speak of transcendent mystery and truth. It is not only our vocation; it is our job. Even when it's the last thing we'd choose to do, we preach anyway. More than that, we preach as best we can, because we know deep in our bones that what we say from the pulpit and how we say it matters. It matters to us and to the people who listen, and it matters to God.

All preachers wish they had time to do justice to this remarkable and awesome responsibility, but such time is rarely afforded. I tell parishioners that preaching is what keeps me believing in miracles. That I have anything at all to offer each week is nothing short of amazing. "You make it seem easy," they say. If only they knew how little I start with and how messy the work can be, surely they would wonder why the task of divine proclamation is entrusted to such a risky process. Why indeed. Saint Paul likens us to earthen containers, holding the great treasure of faith. As containers, he says, we're nothing special. We're like clay jars, so that we never forget that the power belongs to God and does not come from us (2 Corinthians 4:4). All preachers acknowledge, when we're honest, that the power of our words belongs to God. Can Jesus transform a few loaves of bread into a feast? Absolutely. For preachers, that transformation is a weekly event.

Yet, preaching is also work, a discipline like any other, requiring time and attention. We should have little patience for those who take the responsibility of preaching lightly. A sloppy, trite, or boring preacher does as much to discredit the gospel of Christ as an arrogant, self-righteous one. Who else in the community is afforded fifteen to twenty minutes of uninterrupted speech? Who else is given the authority to speak in that space where human souls come in search of God? We had better give the task of preaching the best we have to offer. The trick is to find the balance between taking our work too seriously (a deadly flaw) and not seriously enough. As with all mysteries of grace, preaching is both a gift to be received and something to work at with fear and trembling. It is the hardest work, for which we never will have enough time, and a gift that God freely gives for us to share.

I've come to regard preaching as a spiritual discipline of leadership. It is, first and foremost, a spiritual practice, the means through which I struggle with the most important questions of life and faith. Preaching is a vehicle of grace, one of the most consistent ways I experience the mercy and blessing of God. In preaching I discern meaning and direction for my own future and that of the congregation. As such, the sermon's first gift is always to the preacher.

Preaching is also the gift I give back to God and the community of faith. When I rise before the congregation, I stand at the center of several relationships. I am in relationship with God, our sacred texts, each person listening, and our community as a whole. We are all in relationship with God, our community, and culture. We are in relationship with one another directly and indirectly. We are all affected by world events, sometimes dramatically. If I can give voice to the emotional undercurrent of these many relationships and speak truth from it, what others experience is grace. They get the feeling that I've been following them around all week and speaking the truth they most need to hear. What I'm actually doing is speaking the truth they already know. They hear in my words the voice of their own souls or even the voice of God.

Preaching is not merely a spiritual discipline for the preacher's sake or even that of the individuals gathered on Sunday morning. It is a spiritual discipline of leadership, offered in the context of a community of faith with a common mission of faithfulness to Christ. It serves to inspire and challenge that community to be transformed and empowered by the presence of Christ in their midst. For preaching to serve this crucial community function, it must be connected to all other dimensions of leadership, as the head is to the body. There is an organic relationship between how ministers preach and carry out all other duties of ministry. Preaching is related to how we facilitate meetings, counsel in emergencies, and organize for justice. Words alone do not proclaim the gospel. The authenticity and transparency of our lives and relationships inform preaching, quite apart from how many hours we spend preparing an actual sermon.

Preaching in the context of trusted relationship ensures continuity and consistency of the community's spiritual tone. It gives voice to our collective identity as people of faith, and points to where God is calling us to be. It is a means for collective discernment. Offered in the context of long-term relationship and faithful leadership, preaching is an ongoing dialogue between preacher and congregation in which the insights and experiences of the community find expression. As one preeminent preacher in the Episcopal church, Barbara Brown Taylor, writes, "Preaching is not something an ordained minister does for fifteen minutes on Sundays, but what the whole congregation does all week long; it is a way of approaching the world, and of gleaning God's presence there."[2] Preachers must listen well to preach well, not merely to the words of scripture but to the voices of truth all around.

Preaching is also an event. Something happens in that moment, like an electrical current passing among us. It is not enough to speak of God's love; we need to help others experience it. It's not enough to describe grace or judgment or renewed commitment; our task is to help create the environment in which others can *know God*. The great early twentieth-century preacher, Harry Emerson Fosdick, put it this way: "A pastor has not merely to discuss repentance but to persuade people to repent; not merely to debate the meaning and possibility of Christian faith, but to produce faith in the life of his listeners ... to create in his congregations the thing he is talking about."[3] This is the art of preaching and the power of it. We unite our energies with the Spirit of God, discerning the message to be preached and then offering it with passion and grace, so that others might hear, receive, and respond.

But where does one find the time for such good and lofty work? When does it begin? Is it on Monday morning in the midst of all other work to be done? Is it on Friday, the supposed day off for most clergy and often the first time we have the opportunity to sit quietly? How do we cope with the inevitable crises that crowd our mornings of study? How much time must we spend to preach well, and how best does one use that time?

I write for all those parish pastors and priests who want to preach well, who long to speak with authority, clarity, and humility, and yet who feel, as I do, that there is simply never enough time in the week to do justice to the task. I write for those who feel at times overwhelmed by the responsibilities of our work, who wonder if it is possible, in parish ministry, to live a balanced life. I write from that same place of struggle myself. While preaching is without question the most challenging work that I do, I have come to experience preaching as the place of integration, where the important strands of my life in God and leadership come together. It is an amazing grace. I believe that if we preachers can claim our vocation and trust that God is with us, longing for us to experience the gospel we are called to proclaim, we will speak with quiet authority and compassion. As we experience our own lives as the window through which Christ's love is communicated, we grow in authenticity, transparency, and grace, and through our words, invite others to do the same.

11

1. Garrison Keillor quote from an introduction to a compact disc titled *A Prairie Home Companion 25th Anniversary Celebration.*

2. Barbara Brown Taylor, *The Preaching Life* (Cambridge: The Cowley Fathers, 1993), p. 32.

3. Quoted by Elisabeth Sifton in *The Serenity Prayer: Faith and Politics in Times of Peace and War* (New York: W. W. Norton & Company, 2005), p. 190.

Preaching As Prayer

Many Christians I know have a steady, disciplined prayer life that includes a daily practice of meditation and scripture reading. Parish clergy are rarely among them. I used to have such a practice, honestly, before I was ordained and became a parent. My strongest spiritual memories of young adulthood are of sitting at the breakfast table after an early morning run, reading the Bible, and writing in my journal.

Time moved slowly for me those years. I was lonely and often found myself looking through the windows of other people's lives, wondering when mine would begin. One place I felt at home was in prayer. I loved the simplicity of the daily lectionary in the *Book of Common Prayer*, and I carefully followed its instructions. I found solace reading spiritual books by authors whose memoirs gave me language with which to understand my own life: Dorothy Day's *The Long Loneliness*, Thomas Merton's *The Seven-Story Mountain*, and Emily Griffin's book on adult conversion, *Turning*. Reading was prayer for me, a source of solace and inspiration. Journal writing was also prayer, a practice that demanded honesty and provided release. These daily disciplines of sacred reading and writing sustained me, and I return to them whenever I need to begin again in prayer. Try as I might, however, I cannot maintain them for long. I still keep a journal and read the lectionary, but they are now occasional practices more suited for times away from the normal demands of my life.

In seminary, I attended daily morning and evening prayer. I also practiced other forms of prayer with a small group of friends. We would gather in the evenings for guided meditations and healing prayer. I fell in love with our communal spiritual practice, no doubt intended to prepare us to be priests, and I marveled at the power of spiritual friendship.

As I made the transition into parish ministry, I did my best to maintain the practices that had defined my young adult and seminary life and for several years I kept at them. But in the context of new responsibilities, they soon began to feel like a burden. My life no longer conformed to the monastic rhythms of morning and evening chapel. With a full-time job and young children at home, I couldn't even ensure a quiet half hour before dawn. Those first years of ordained and married life were disorienting as I adjusted to changes in identity, daily routine, and the many tasks of congregational ministry. The disorientation was compounded by the fact that my cherished spiritual disciplines no longer *worked*. It was embarrassing, even shameful to admit that as a priest I wasn't sure I knew how to pray.

The question of integrity began to take on real urgency. I was busier than I had ever been, living on little sleep, torn in my loyalties as a parent and minister, and often overwhelmed by the emotional complexity of relationships in every realm of my life.

In a lifesaving moment, a friend mentioned her studies with a certain rabbi in Washington DC, Edwin Friedman, who had written a book about congregational leadership. "You might see if you can join one of his seminars," she said.

I bought Friedman's book, *Generation to Generation*, and started to read, understanding less than half of what he wrote, but knowing, nonetheless, that I had found something important. Gathering my courage, I called Friedman and asked to join his seminars for clergy.

Friedman wasn't particularly receptive. "We've just started a group," he said, "and the next one won't begin until sometime next year." I wonder if he heard my heart sink as I struggled to ask, "Is there any way I might begin sooner?" He was silent for a moment. "Have you read my book?" he asked, sounding slightly irritated. "I'm reading it now," I said. "Do you understand it?" "Yes," I lied. He agreed to let me enroll and a month later I found myself traveling to Bethesda, Maryland. It was a journey I would take twice a year for the next decade.

Rabbi Friedman taught me, alongside an entire generation of clergy, that it was possible to live an integrated life as a congregational leader. It wasn't easy, but it was possible. Such a life, he said, required continual work at self-definition in the context of relationships in three distinct arenas: your family of origin, your immediate family, and the relationship dynamics of the congregation you serve. He claimed the issues and struggles in all three were the same. You needn't divide yourself into component parts and endless roles. You are who you are wherever you are, and you have a unique role to play in each relationship system of your life. If you do this, you needn't ever worry about sermon preparation. The self is an inexhaustible supply of sermons.

The self is an inexhaustible supply of sermons. Slowly I began to experience what Friedman described: sermon preparation as a vehicle for self-definition and integration. While writing a sermon was without question the greatest source of anxiety in my week, I recognized all the characteristics of spiritual practice. To prepare a sermon, I needed to engage scripture and meditate on its meaning. I needed time to think, study, and write. Most importantly, I needed to listen to my life and the lives of those around me, holding the words of scripture as I pondered what, if anything, God might have to say. Amazingly the words came, like manna, enough for the day.

Then there was the sermon delivery itself: standing before a community with text in hand, offering the words and sensing God's power passing through them. It was, and remains, the greatest mystery. I've learned that even the terrible sermons — the ones that don't come together, ramble on forever, or feel empty and flat — are not without value. They teach humility, for starters, and the lessons of failure. They also demonstrate with startling clarity how creative the Holy Spirit can be in the distance between the preacher's mouth and listener's ears.

The most important insight I have learned in congregational ministry is this: The process of preparing and giving sermons is a preacher's form of prayer. Undisputedly, preaching is a discipline. We preach whether we want to or not. To our astonishment, preaching can also be a gift, transforming the burden of work into a consistent place of encounter with God. Preaching provides a way for us to respond to God in the context of our vocation.

What a relief to recognize as spiritual practice one of the most significant responsibilities of ministry and something that connects us to the rest of life, too. We don't need to set aside unreasonable hours for sermon preparation. Preparation is part of everything we

15

do. Rather than further compartmentalize our lives in order to make room for the task, preparing a sermon has an integrating, even simplifying effect. It is our practice and our prayer. Even more, it can become our passion, the art form given us to express the greatest of mysteries — God's way with us and ours with God.

Preaching as prayer begins with trust. Implausible as it feels, the act of preaching — proclaiming God's word in a particular place to a particular people — flows from God's desire to guide us and provide us the words and power we need. This sense of a creative endeavor with God is at the heart of preaching. The energy and insight doesn't come from us alone. This is easy to forget when Sunday morning looms and we need to come to come up with something to say.

What is prayer like in that moment? The writer, Ann Lamott, sits before her computer each morning and prays that she does not get in the way of what needs to be written. My prayers, when I remember to say them, tend to be variations on the same request: *Please help. I don't have enough. I don't know how the pieces fit. I don't know where to begin. I need help.* Invariably something happens to move the process along, not always on my timetable, or even in ways that I recognize at first. But that *something happening* is trustworthy. It's what makes the experience of preaching feel like prayer.

Yet God doesn't dictate sermons. We also need to be faithful to the habits of life that preaching requires. Preaching takes practice, like any other art form. In his novel, *Blues Lessons,* Robert Hellenga tells the story of a young man who falls in love with the music played by the farm workers who come up to his family's Michigan farm each summer to pick crops. He learns how to play the guitar and seeks to find his way in the rough, hard-drinking world of music-makers. One of his mentors tells him, "It's not drinking whiskey that makes you a bluesman, and it ain't selling your soul to the devil. What makes you a bluesman is playing the blues."[1] What makes preachers is preaching, as often and as best we can, practicing the scales of our vocation with as much diligence as any other artist.

For me, the scales of preaching include approaching life as a perpetual learner, engaging the scripture texts of each sermon, paying attention to the flow of life within and around me, writing down everything that comes to me, and finally seeking clarity through the long process of revision. The last night before a sermon and again in the early morning, I am writing and rewriting, often up to the last minute. That's what faithfulness to the process of preaching requires, as I do my best to communicate the gospel with which I am entrusted. In the final hours, preparing to preach feels nothing like a burden. It's a gift of creative expression that I want nothing more than to complete as best as I can.

Lastly, preaching as prayer requires honesty. Jesus came to bear witness to the truth and calls us to do the same, beginning with an honest assessment of ourselves. In a small book of prayers titled *Primary Speech*, Ann and Barry Ulanov wrote, "In prayer we say who we in fact are — not who we should be, nor who we wish we were, but who we are. All prayer begins with this confession."[2] Preaching also demands that we bring all of who we are to God: what we're thinking and feeling; all of our doubts, fears, and performance anxiety; our hopes and disappointments. There's an element of confession in preaching, as with prayer. We can't hide our sins and shortcomings as we set about to preach in God's name. Nor does false humility serve us, for we will need to develop and utilize all our strengths. When preparing to preach, we do our best to acknowledge our failings, give thanks for our gifts, and *begin*.

---

1. Robert Hellenga, *Blues Lessons* (New York: Scribner, 2002), p. 183.

2. Ann and Barry Ulanov, *Primary Speech* (Atlanta: John Knox Press, 1982), p. 3.

17

Building The Foundation, Part One: Preaching As We Live And Lead

The preaching process begins long before we sit down to read the scripture passages for a given Sunday. It begins with our approach to life and ministry. How do we live each day? What is the rhythm of our work? Where does preaching fit in the tapestry of responsibilities we carry? There isn't a blueprint for ministers to follow or universal answers to the great questions of our vocation. No matter what our systems of authority are, others cannot define our vocation for us. We must determine for ourselves what we believe we are called by God to do and to preach. It takes years for such clarity to emerge, but simply holding the question in our hearts ensures that our preaching will have the ring of authenticity. When we preach it will be *our* voice speaking.

We do ourselves a great disservice by attempting to live by another's lights or speak another person's truth. While we can learn from others, there is no escaping the hard work of finding our own truth to live and proclaim. Thomas Merton once cautioned both poets and monks against the dangers of imitation in words that preachers are also wise to heed:

> *Many poets are not poets for the same reason that many religious men are not saints: They never succeeded in being themselves ... They wear out their minds and bodies in a hopeless endeavor to have somebody else's experiences or write somebody else's poems or possess somebody else's sanctity.*[1]

It takes courage to believe that God has called us to the pulpit to be ourselves. Yet we begin by simply speaking from the heart. "Just talk to us," a kind woman counseled me as I prepared to preach my first sermon as an ordained person. What she meant was, "Don't put on airs." It was, and remains, good advice. To speak of our own experience of grace, or simply the search for it, within a particular community at a unique moment in time is the task and the gift of preaching.

19

Preaching also serves a particular function in worship and in the spiritual journey of a faith community. We offer hospitality and welcome by the tone we establish in the pulpit. We give voice and legitimacy to the questions and struggles of the people who come, as well as challenge their assumptions about God. We become the official spokesperson for the community's ministry.

Three words describe for me the preaching function in worship: *presence*, *tone*, and *vision*. A ministry of presence is simply one of showing up, being present to the mystery of grace, the community of faith, the larger society in which our community is placed, and the realities, both gifts and limitations, of my own life. Presence assumes an active spirit, engaged heart, and attentive mind. It doesn't mean that I'm present at every event, know every person, or am available 24 hours a day. It simply means that I am invested in the system as a whole, aware of how the pieces fit together, and how the congregation functions in the context of its environment. It means that I care about everyone's experience of faith and community, even if I spend more time attending to the big picture than to the details of a given initiative. It means that I am engaged with the parish's life and connected to all parts of it.

To be present in the pulpit is to be mindful of all that converges in that moment and respectful of God's unique relationship with each person. It ensures that members of the congregation will hear me speaking to them, not at them. Preaching from a place of presence requires humility, honesty, and an earnest desire to be present to God as God is revealed in our midst. It strives for calm and passion, depth and humor, and an intentional yet light touch. It isn't our presence that matters most, but rather how we facilitate the congregation's receptivity to God's presence in the person of Jesus Christ and the workings of grace.

Tone describes the mood or feel of a church when a person walks in the door, the emotional and spiritual atmosphere of a community — its heart and soul. A primary function of spiritual leadership is to help establish and nourish a healthy and relaxed tone in the church. Such a tone allows us to be at peace with ourselves and open to the Spirit of God. It establishes clear emotional boundaries of trust and accountability, and yet allows for human nature and the inevitable mistakes and failures in life. It promotes maturity, laughter, and joy, and yet is not afraid of tears and sorrow in response to life's hardships.

In his book on congregational leadership, *Generation to Generation*, Rabbi Edwin Friedman writes of the power of leadership to lower anxiety in a community. He observes that when anxiety rises in a community, people's capacity to hear one another and deal with difficulty diminishes. Humor all but disappears. But when the threshold of anxiety is brought down, people saying the exact same words can hear one another better, and they are more open to the voice of God speaking to them through their spiritual tradition.[2] Paying attention to spiritual tone informs preaching at every turn. How we sound from the pulpit — the tone of our voice and the emotional undercurrent of our words — affects how people hear and experience the gospel.

Vision is the most important leadership function to affect preaching. It is "big picture" thinking, daring to ask the important questions — probing why we do what we do and defining our most important work: what it means to live as a community of faith. Vision is both lofty and practical. To speak from a place of vision about the importance of one area of the community's life and mission — children's education, for example, or justice work — is to make the connections to the community as a whole and why it matters to everyone, thus ensuring greater ownership and support. Yet vision involves casting one's gaze to the horizon, beyond where we are, beyond even what we can see, and attempt to give voice where God might be leading us.

Vision is the work of inspiration and relationship, requiring time, patience, and careful listening, both to God and to the people. There is nothing to be served by placing a vision before a community that has no connection to the community's sense of itself. Nothing will be accomplished, except clergy exhaustion, by acting as a visionary alone. Words, no matter how inspiring, mean little if we don't also invest in the painstaking work of vision's fulfillment. Vision involves periods of waiting, group discernment, and reinterpretation along the way. It requires us to ask questions that require time and struggling to answer. What does it mean to wait on the Lord? Will we recognize the vision when it comes? How will we live in the messy stages of vision's realization?

All three dimensions — presence, tone, and vision — ask us to be active and engaged in the life of the community we serve, attentive to the concerns of our hearts, and aware of the world around us. They ensure that we don't speak with a preaching tone, different from our voice in other settings. Preaching allows us the privilege and opportunity to reflect prayerfully on the important issues of our time in light of our spiritual texts and the Holy Spirit's work in the world. We offer our insights in the first person — the best that we can say at this moment in time — not to convince or manipulate, but to stimulate thought, discussion, and response in those who listen. In this way, preaching creates space for the Spirit of God to act and for the people of God to think for themselves.

---

1. Quoted in *The Life You Save May Be Your Own* by Paul Elie (New York: Ferrar, Straus and Giroux, 2003), p. 186.

2. Edwin Friedman, *Generation to Generation* (New York: Guilford Press, 1985), especially chapter 9, "Leadership and Self in a Congregational Family," pp. 220-249.

Building The Foundation, Part Two: Preaching As Lifelong Study

Clergy were once considered among the best-educated members of their communities, the ones to turn to for counsel on a wide range of concerns. While no longer granted such venerated status, clergy are nonetheless expected to be thoughtful and learned people. It is a legitimate expectation, rooted in our lifelong devotion to scripture and responsibility to relate to all aspects of life. Just as Jesus drew his parables and metaphors from the real-life circumstances of those listening to him, so we draw upon knowledge from a wide range of subjects when we speak of God's presence and concern in our world.

Indeed, what we think we should know as pastors can be a cause of considerable anxiety. In seminary we studied the Bible in depth, the Hebrew and Christian texts, in addition to theology, church history, ethics, liturgy, and pastoral care. We were taught by professors who were passionate about their fields. We were inspired by them and we became passionate ourselves, determined after seminary to maintain our knowledge in key academic disciplines.

There are many subjects that we didn't study in seminary but wish we had: business administration, psychology, community organizing, and computer science. These are all essential in running a parish, which functions at once like a small business, neighborhood school, community center, and extended family. Beyond seminary, we need on-the-job training in countless skills that we call upon daily. How can we learn what we need to know about reaching those not attending church, or new music and liturgical styles, the importance of small group ministry, and how to prevent sexual misconduct in our congregations, to name only a few of the concerns facing church leaders today?

Clergy are also expected, rightfully so, to have a grasp of the issues in our local communities, as well as some perspective on world events. The church does not exist in a bubble, and we as leaders need to pay attention to what surrounds us. While some would prefer their clergy never mention politics, scripture makes it clear that we who speak in God's name must address the pressing social concerns of our time. Prophetic speech is nonnegotiable, yet we must navigate carefully, with full awareness of our biases. We need to study and to listen, allowing our perspectives to be broadened with insights from across a wide spectrum of views.

Finally, there are the spiritual disciplines at the heart of our vocation as pastors and priests. Not only do we need to know how to pray ourselves, we must teach others. We need to know how to deal with conflict and human imperfection, anger and hurt. We need to know how to forgive and how to make difficult and discerning decisions. In short, we need to know how to *live*. We don't necessarily need answers for life's great mysteries, but our calling, above all, is to embrace and ponder the questions deeply and have something to say about them when we speak. That is what people want to hear from us most of all.

If we devoted a lifetime only to study there would be insufficient time to fulfill our expectations and thirst for knowledge. Like other areas of ministry, our life of learning can only be held in balance with other claims on our time. We need to study and learn strategically, finding ways to distinguish among the countless sources of information what is essential for us. Insufficient time is not a license for abdication. Good preaching, and leadership in general, rests upon a life committed to learning and growth. We can't preach well on a diet of junk food, nor can we draw resources in the weekly pressure to write a sermon sufficient for wisdom. Fortunately, most clergy I know *like* to study; they enjoy learning and expanding their horizons. The question isn't whether or not to study but what to study and how to go about it. The issue is how to decide among all that could be learned what is best to learn. What fields are essential? How does one maintain a discipline of study when other responsibilities crowd from other sides?

I am convinced that the best way to discern what we need to learn is by following our hearts. We can't know everything. We can't keep up with all matters of importance. Thus, the question becomes: What do we need to engage now, for our own soul's sake? What subjects seem to claim us? What isn't a burden for us to study, but a joy? We can trust the Holy Spirit's guidance here. Part of discovering our voice in the pulpit involves going where our concerns, interests, and passions take us. For what we care about, no matter the subject, will infuse our preaching with life.

A colleague of mine is passionate about music and trains. Before seminary he was a professional musician, trained in the classical tradition. He also loves everything there is to know and experience about trains: riding trains, building models in his basement, and studying the history of trains in this country. Of particular interest to him is the role trains played in American migration, especially of African Americans moving north after the Civil War and in the early twentieth century. I have heard him preach, drawing upon imagery from both of his great loves and leaving the congregation breathless. His enthusiasm and knowledge inform his preaching seamlessly and authentically. Such is the gift of passion.

Barbara Brown Taylor, so fine a preacher that many of us wish we could simply read her sermons from the pulpit, wrote in her first of many books of her love of the Bible:

> *My first serious study of the Bible began in seminary, where I read Genesis in Hebrew and discovered a whole new world. Each day's vocabulary list opened new windows. Adam got his name from* adamah, *the dust of the earth. At least one of the worlds for God,* elohim, *was plural. The word for "eye" also meant "fountain of water," and the word for "rib" could also be interpreted "side room," which told me that Eve was created from one whole side of Adam's nature.... After that, I was hooked. I couldn't read the simplest passage in the Old and New Testaments without wondering what the words really meant. All of this excited me, because there was clearly more to the Bible than I had ever expected, and exploring it demanded more of me as well.*[1]

Her sermons flow passionately from her love of the Bible, taking her listeners to great depths of insight, humor, and identification with biblical characters and their struggles.

My passions plunge me into the mysterious waters of human nature, the study of human beings. I love history, social sciences, biographies, and fiction. I love the Bible for its human qualities as much as its divine inspiration. My first serious study of the Bible also began in seminary, and I was delighted to discover real people in its pages, full of foibles and doubts, broken and often foolish characters that God nonetheless loves and seeks out for divine purpose.

When I study the Bible, I'm drawn to the dialogue, the questions, the struggles, and the context in which God's presence or absence is experienced. That's what I look for. In past years, I've been drawn to the study of psychology, quoting enough of it from the pulpit that the psychologists in the congregation, some secretly wanting to be priests, wondered if I secretly wanted to be a psychologist. Other years I have immersed myself in history and the examples of my sermons were drawn from various historical periods of our nation, often with surprising relevance. When my children were young, I read mostly children's books and watched the Public Broadcasting Service (PBS) on television, and my sermons were sprinkled with examples from *Winnie the Pooh* and *Sesame Street*. Paying attention to our life and following our life's passion gives us, as preachers, our unique connections to the gospel.

We can't rely on our interests and sources alone, however, when cultivating a lifelong discipline of preaching. We need help to see beyond our own horizons. One relatively painless way to expand our body of knowledge is to rely on the work others have done. I am, for example, a collector of interesting quotes. I write down everything that I come across that strikes me as important. When I finish a well-written novel, I record all the passages that moved me. I subscribe to anthologies of poetry and spirituality and several newspapers. I selectively search the internet. I also ask others to share with me the interesting things that they come across in their reading and work. These are disciplines for life as well as preaching. It is essential to consider other people's ideas and draw from other sources so that our leadership is informed by deep and varied wells of wisdom and life experience.

There are aspects of lifelong learning that are simply fun: watching films, reading novels, engaging in good conversation, and delighting in children as they play. Part of our vocation is to think deeply about what is on everyone's mind and to hold our lives up to the light of Christ in search of meaning and grace. It may not feel like sermon preparation to watch all the movies nominated for Oscars in a given year, to see a special on PBS, to spend an afternoon coaching your daughter's basketball team, or to finally read the novel everyone is talking about, but somewhere among them lies the story that will one day become the perfect sermon illustration. It isn't as if everything we do is work, but our work is drawn from *all* that we do. That sense of connection allows us to relax and trust that we will be given all that we need to preach authentically and well, week after week.

1. Barbara Brown Taylor, *The Preaching Life* (Cambridge: Cowley Publications, 1993), pp. 56-56.

Beginning In Earnest: Letting God Speak Through The Texts

When preparing to preach a particular sermon, the most obvious task is to engage the scripture texts chosen for the occasion. In some traditions, it is the preacher's responsibility to select biblical texts and themes for each Sunday. In others, the texts are chosen in advance. I preach according to the Revised Common Lectionary, a three-year cycle of biblical texts organized around the liturgical calendar and seasons of the Christian year. The lectionary is a gift of structure and theme. Lectionary-based preachers have great freedom in preaching, provided we remain grounded in the texts. Lectionary preaching often feels like writing a poem within boundaries, more like a sonnet, not free verse. Within the parameters given us from the appointed day, we are free to speak from our hearts.

The trap for lectionary-based preachers is over-exegesis of the texts, as if our tasks were to explain their meaning. But we are not leading Bible study from the pulpit. We are proclaiming the gospel of Christ, interpreting biblical texts in light of Christ's life and presence among us. Of course we are to approach the Bible intelligently and prayerfully and invite our listeners to do the same; nonetheless, it's important to remember that people are hungry not for the Bible, but for God. The texts and our interpretation of them are in service to God, as we give words to the mystery and power of God in and among the community gathered.

I begin my engagement with scripture unaided, as commentaries and other biblical guides can be distracting. I will take up study later, but initially I simply allow the scriptures to take up residence within me as a form of devotion or personal inquiry. Ruthanna Hook, professor of homiletics at Virginia Seminary, suggests that her students memorize the texts on which they are to preach and recite them all week long as a mantra, a discipline that I have begun. As I put in a load of laundry, drive to visit a parishioner in the hospital, or conduct a vestry meeting, I hold the passages in my heart. I pay attention to my initial reactions, the questions that surface, and what God might be saying to me through the texts in the context of current struggles and blessings. If circumstances allow, I will ask others to read and reflect on the passages. In general, however, I invite God to speak to me first, as I ponder the meaning of sacred word and truth.

This first step of engagement and prayerful free association with scripture is the foundation upon which all preaching with integrity is built. It ensures that our words will be offered in a spirit of humility and self-reflection. It isn't generally advisable to share these early ruminations, particularly if they are personal and directly related to immediate struggles. The energy of them, however, informs the entire sermon, and people will respond with energy of their own.

When we allow the word of God to speak to us first, we will never sound judgmental, distant, or spiritually superior from the pulpit, because we speak from our own soul's truth. If there is a prophetic word to be preached, we will preach as ones who stand underneath its truth alongside everyone else. If we preach repentance, we begin from our own need to repent. If we preach of the love and mercy of God, we will speak as ones who hunger for that love and mercy, and on occasion, have received it. If we preach on the unsolvable mysteries of life, such as human suffering and how faith in a loving God can either die or thrive in the face of it, we won't offer platitudes but rather speak humbly, knowing that often our task is to honor the questions rather than answer them.

It isn't easy to discern when to include personal insights, the fruits of our early prayer, in a sermon. I'm convinced that it's impossible to know what to share at the beginning of the preparation process. A common mistake of preaching, however, occurs right here, in the early stages, when we assume that the congregation needs to hear every insight that moves us forward.

The author, Annie Dillard, advises fellow writers to throw away their beginning work. She also acknowledges that it's not easy to do:

Several delusions weaken the writer's resolve to throw away work. If he has read his pages too often, those pages will have a necessary quality, the ring of the inevitable, like poetry known by heart ... He may retain those pages if they possess some virtues, such as power in themselves, though they lack the cardinal virtue, which is pertinence to, and unity with, the book's thrust. [1]

The perils in preaching are similar. Much of our preparation in the early stages of preaching belongs in the privacy of our own relationship to Christ. It takes courage and a ruthless bit of editing later on to leave them there.

There are times, however, when I will include my initial responses to a sermon text, if they serve the final message well: I began one sermon, based on a passage from the book of Leviticus, like this:

I wonder what it would look like for us to be faithful to the ancient commandment, "You shall not reap to the very edges of your field." Whatever it looks like, I'm certain that I'm not good at it. There's something about my life that always seems to take me to the edge of whatever I'm doing. So when I read this passage from Leviticus earlier this week, it went straight to my heart and I've been thinking about it ever since.

Another sermon, based on the parable of the man thrown out of a wedding banquet for wearing the wrong clothes, I began:

Have you ever walked into a party that you thought was a formal affair only to discover that everyone else was in blue jeans, or you were the one in jeans when everyone else was in elegant black? Do you attend the kind of school or work in an environment where people assess each other according to style and money? Or is your social circle decidedly anti-style, with a uniform all its own? I've always admired people who don't care about such things, and I try to be like that myself, but I'm not. In my heart, I always want to know what other people are wearing. Even in my days of intentional non-conformity, I was most comfortable in the company of other non-conformists, conforming exactly to what non-conformists wear.

The value of early ruminations can't be measured, however, on whether or not they wind up in the final sermon. They are simply how we begin, our food for the journey. They enable us to preach to others with a sense of being fed ourselves. It may be that the message spoken to us will be an explicit part of what we preach to others, or it may be part of the emotional energy that carries our passion and faith, unspoken yet infusing each word. The gift is given to us. How much to share that gift with others is a decision we make later on.

---

1. Annie Dillard, *The Writing Life* (New York: HarperPerennial, 1989), p. 6.

Paying Attention

After reading and ruminating on the scripture passage, the next step of sermon preparation feels like a scavenger hunt or a search for puzzle pieces to fit together. In one account of the miracle of loaves and fishes, Jesus instructs his disciples to gather up the fragments left over, so that none may be lost (John 6:12). Likewise in preaching, there is great spiritual power in gathering up fragments of wisdom and truth. As I go about life and ministry, I pay attention to the bits and pieces of insight that come my way. I don't try to put them in any order or try to make connections at first — I simply gather them up.

This is when I refer to biblical commentaries and other preaching aids. I might read an anthology or essay related to the topic emerging in my mind. If I need to do research, I make time for it now, trying to stay focused and also open to unexpected ideas that I may uncover. I follow any lead, both internally and externally. I listen to the radio. I pay attention to what people say in conversation, attuned to the vignettes that might fit an emerging theme. I take to heart the memories and associations that rise from the surface of my unconscious.

Much of this work takes place in the background of my life. No one would suspect that I am thinking about a sermon. I'm simply paying attention, looking for connections, wondering how the themes of a particular biblical passage resonate with the undercurrent of my life and the lives of those around me. It is a playful time, guided by imagination and the realities of a given week. Some weeks I have ample opportunity to read and research; during many others, however, I need to rely on what comes my way as I face the demands and concerns I cannot ignore. Here is where the notion of sermon preparation takes on broad implications — it becomes part of everything that I must tend to in a given week.

Relatively early in the process, I make a few key decisions about what kind of sermon it will be. Will it be rooted in history or contemporary experience? How do I best communicate the scripture's core truth? Do I need to study up on a particular area of theology and include it for its relevance and insight? Or will this be, as is most often the case, a sermon drawn from ordinary things to convey the extraordinary workings of God?

The ideas and connections that come to mind in this gathering-up-the-fragments phase often come as a surprise. While playing racquetball at a local YMCA and trying to work out a sermon on the temptation to focus on the attributes of God that appeal to us and ignore those that don't, I remembered a joke I had heard years before that served as the sermon's introduction:

> *A rabbi tells the story of Moses going up the mountain to receive the law of God. God hands Moses the Ten Commandments. Moses reads them and then asks, "Could you make it five?"*

> *Or in a different version of the same story, Moses goes up the mountain and God hands him twenty commandments. Moses says, "Look, you've got to narrow these down to ten." God thinks for a moment, and then replies, "All right. But the one about adultery stays in."*

From there I took a more serious tone, citing the difficult passages of scripture I would edit out if I could, before making a case for honoring all of scripture as part of our sacred, albeit messy and very human texts. All of our lives as well, even the parts we wish we could leave on the editing floor.

Another time, while driving, I heard the last half of a radio interview with a newly published author. The author said something about the nature of courage that spoke directly to what I was struggling with for my sermon that week. I pulled over and began taking notes. When I got home I called a bookstore to reserve a copy of his book, and while it would be months before I read it, the radio interview and the title itself figured heavily in my sermon:

> *We're often drawn to religion out of a vague sense that it would be a good thing to have, like life insurance, or out of guilt, that we should be doing more or living better than we are. No doubt these things are true, at*

least in part. But I believe that what God desires most to give us is courage, *courage to face what life brings us, and the strength we need to live in good and meaningful ways....*

Certainly part of the courage God longs to give is that which enables us to participate in the salvation of the world. We can't respond to everything, but with courage we can respond to some things. "Be strong, do not fear!" Live well. Love well. Who knows, if through our efforts, imperfect as they are, we might *save another's life? Who knows? The life we save, with our imperfect love, may be our own. (This last sentence was inspired by the title of a book by Paul Elie,* The Life You Save May Be Your Own.*)*

Once over lunch, a parishioner, who is a painter and art teacher, gave me the perfect metaphor for a certain aspect of faithfulness. I was working on a sermon about what faith feels like when we don't have a clear vision for the future or when we've lost our bearings. In describing her work, she supplied the language I was looking for:

Painting involves risk, moving beyond the familiar toward what we cannot see. It's like approaching a corner before actually making the turn, going forward without knowing what lies beyond the curve. It's like sailing beyond the horizon, toward the shore of a distant land. In the words of the French writer, Andre Gide, "One doesn't discover new lands without consenting to lose sight of the shore for a very long time."

Finding that missing piece for a sermon in a conversation, radio show, or private memory is a marvelously affirming spiritual experience. It's often the insight that holds an entire sermon together or the illustration that everyone remembers long after the sermon itself is forgotten.

There are a few things to keep in mind during the gathering up stage of sermon preparation. The first is that we will only know which of the many fragments we gather belong in a particular sermon as we work on the clarity of our message. In the beginning, they may all seem important; in the end, we may use only a few, as we become clearer about what we're trying to say.

The great professor of homiletics, Fred B. Craddock, suggests we divide our preparation process into two distinct parts. In the first part, we determine the message itself; in the second, we decide how to communicate it. The first part is rooted in good scripture study, reading a passage in its own context, and then placing it in the context of the congregation. The second half involves shaping the message with an eye to unity, form, and presentation.[1]

While Craddock's model is commendable, my own preparation is rarely that clean or clear. I often don't discover the sermon's central message until I am well into the process of writing it. Craddock is right to insist, however, that before we step into the pulpit we should be as clear as possible about our central message. Every word, illustration, and story of our sermon must be held to its light. Such evaluation is, of course, impossible if we don't know what our core message is, and sadly we often don't. The most common weakness in preaching is lack of clarity and organizing purpose. Sermons without clarity become like the proverbial kitchen sink — we include every idea that occurs to us. No matter how interesting those ideas are, without a cohesive framework, they do not serve gospel proclamation well.

On the other hand, in the gathering stage we do well to cast our nets wide. One definition of brilliance is the ability to see connections between seemingly disparate realities. There's a reason why you and I are drawn to particular ideas and insights during sermon preparation. Our task is to hold all of them together and allow the chemistry between them to speak. There will be time in final editing to remove what ultimately doesn't belong, but we may need the full mix of ideas to move us to a place of greater clarity.

Sermon preparation can be messy, but a certain amount of messiness is part of the creative process. As Anne Lamott writes, "Clutter is wonderfully fertile ground — you can still discover new treasures under all those piles, clean things up, edit things out, fix things, get a grip ... Tidiness makes me think of held breath, of suspended animation, while writing needs to breathe and move."[2] Even if we don't wind up using everything, the stories or ideas left behind in editing this sermon may fit in another.

Finally, we need to be prepared to respond to a major event or crisis that occurs during the week before we preach. All crises are disruptions, and as preachers we will experience them that way, a dramatic shift that tosses aside whatever sermon preparation we have begun. When something has shaken the world, no matter the scale, the preaching task is to respond, even if it means starting over and staying up all Saturday night to do it.

Major crises or life-transforming events don't happen often, but when they do, we know it. They may be restricted to the congregation itself, such as a fire in the building or the sudden death of a young person (both of which have happened in the congregation I serve). It could be an event confined to a particular community or one with global repercussions, such as the death of astronauts returning from space, the horrors of September 11, or the devastation of Hurricane Katrina. What distinguishes these events from more prolonged community or public issues (that we must also address in sermons) is their suddenness. Like a thief in the night, something intrudes upon us and profoundly shakes the ground upon which we stand. Our churches will be fuller on the Sunday after such an event, and as the ones called to proclaim the gospel of Christ, we must dig deep within ourselves to find something to say.

On a beautiful autumn Friday in late October 2002, I took a break from writing my sermon to have lunch with a parishioner. On the way to the restaurant I heard the first of several anguished broadcasts about an airplane crash in northern Minnesota. When I arrived, I learned that Senator Paul Wellstone, a beloved political figure in Minnesota and in liberal circles throughout the country, was on the plane, along with his wife, daughter, and several members of his staff. Quiet descended among the restaurant patrons as a news station confirmed that there were no survivors.

I left the restaurant in a daze and went home and packed my bag for a two-day statewide convention of our church. Even though I had little time to work on my sermon and I had no idea what I would say from the pulpit, I knew that it would be about Senator

Wellstone. A large percentage of the congregation I serve is active politically, including some in elected office. Sunday morning would feel like a funeral. I needed to be prepared.

All day Saturday as I pretended to listen to the speakers at the convention, I read newspapers and gathered in my mind all that I could think of to say about Senator Wellstone. I left the convention at 10 p.m., went home, and began to write, relying heavily that night on the grace of God and lots of caffeine. The opening paragraph was the only piece to remain from my original sermon. I was grateful for it, as the beginning of a sermon I could not have even imagined only days before.

> *Ralph Waldo Emerson, the nineteenth-century poet, used to greet old friends with the question, "What has become clear to you since last we met?" If someone were to ask you or me that question, it would be quite a compliment. For it assumes that we are searching for clarity, wrestling with matters of consequence in an effort to gain greater insight and understanding.*
>
> *What has become clear to you since last we met? Clarity, which is the recognition of truth, doesn't come to us all at once, in a whole piece, to take in and be done with. Rather it comes gradually, in time. Our capacity to receive truth and insight also grows in time, as indeed, as human beings are not realized all at once, but in time. We grow and truth grows in us by increments.*
>
> *Of course, things happen that change us and shift our perspective on the world. In a moment it happens. In a moment, a great man and political leader dies, along with his family and close associates. It happens in a moment. What has become clear to you now?*

From there I gave a eulogy for Paul Wellstone, public servant and friend to many of the congregation. It was the most well-received sermon I preached that year, in large measure because I spoke to the shock and grief that all felt in the moment when a beloved's life abruptly ends.

Paying attention to the events and themes that converge in a given week helps unify and integrate our lives as leaders, pastors, and preachers. All are part of a mysterious whole. It is not an over-statement to say that as preachers we are preparing for our next sermon at every moment, whether we realize it or not. For as we listen to the undercurrents of life within and around us, we receive what we ourselves need to hear and can then to share with others.

Major, unexpected events make the decision of what to preach relatively easy. The work is harder, but the task is clear. In the less dramatic rhythms of what we consider normal life, the choices are many and more difficult to choose between. Whenever we preach, however, we need to hold in balance the messages we receive in our own prayers, what we glean from the fragments we gather, and finally, what we know of the congregation to whom we preach. Outside the context of relationship, all that we offer, no matter how insightful, cannot be received. Relationships are an essential ingredient to add to the mix of sermon preparation.

----

1. Fred B. Craddock, *Preaching* (Nashville: Abingdon Press, 1985), p. 153.

2. Anne Lamott, *Bird by Bird: Some Instructions on Writing and Life* (New York: Anchor Books, 1995), p. 29.

Who Will Hear What We Preach?

Relationships are at the heart of preaching. We begin with our own relationship to God and our personal encounter with a biblical text. We engage God's word in the context of our own lives and struggles. Yet preaching is not private devotion. It is a community event, a particular moment in which a constellation of relationships comes together. To preach well we need to consider the people who will hear the sermons we preach. There is no greater influence on the tone and content of my sermons than my relationship to the congregation and the time I spend thinking about particular people as I prepare for Sunday morning.

How well do we know the people to whom we preach? What, specifically, do we know about their questions, concerns, and joys? I've preached to the same congregation for over fifteen years, and in many ways I know the people well. I know the neighborhoods in which they live, the cultural patterns to which they respond, and the socio-economic categories to which they belong. Yet no congregation is static. People move in and out, and even those who remain all their lives are not the same year after year. Those who gather on Sunday morning hear our sermons in the context of their particular strengths and weaknesses, anxieties and hopes. Fred Craddock describes those who fill our churches, "They are all looking for a place to stand, a place that feels like home."[1] Yet all experience that longing in their unique way. What we know of the breadth and complexity of people's lives will influence what we say to them in the name of God.

The church I serve is made up of families of all kinds, many with young children squirming in the pew. Most arrive at church more than a bit frazzled, barely making it in time for the last verse of the opening hymn. Others have no children, and among them are some who wish they did. Some are past the age of children at home and long for a bit more quiet in church and others are single, by circumstance or choice. Children and young people are also part of the congregation. Children listen to sermons, if not to the words, then certainly to the emotional energy reverberating from

41

the pulpit. Adolescents, if not bored to tears, will listen intently. As I prepare, I consider how the word of God might speak to them all. Some in the congregation have strong and steady relationships. They are the couples and families others turn to for support and inspiration, yet even the strongest relationships can be fragile. Some come to church looking for relationships to fill an aching loneliness; others come to heal their broken hearts. Everyone in the congregation knows someone whose primary relationship is unraveling. All children know what the word "divorce" means. Still others are on the verge of falling in love, with all its anticipation and joy. What might the gospel say across such diversity?

Most people in my church are physically healthy, but not all. Some are struggling with life-threatening disease. Almost everyone comes to church praying for someone who is sick. Most are financially secure, but not all. On any given Sunday, someone in the congregation has recently received a layoff notice or worries about the prospect of one. Surely someone spent at least one sleepless night wondering how to pay the mortgage or credit card bills, while another might have spent that same night planning a vacation to the Caribbean. Still another lost sleep wondering how to respond to the overwhelming disparity between the rich and poor of our world. As I prepare, I ponder how one message might reach across such varied and deeply personal experiences.

Many in my church are politically liberal and active in a variety of political and social causes, as am I. They want to hear a relevant gospel assuring them that God cares about justice and that Jesus expects his followers to care about others. It is a gospel that I also believe must be preached and lived. Yet there are others in the congregation, equally dedicated, who don't want to hear political sermons when they come to church, some because they disagree with me and others because they long for church to be a place set apart from polarizing public debates. Surely the church is to be a place of respite as well as challenge. Which impulse do I heed — the prophetic or the pastoral — and when?

It's unrealistic to assume that we can reach all people with every sermon we preach. The scriptural texts themselves have particular truths to uphold, some more challenging or pastoral than others. Moreover, our perspectives and life experiences limit us. We can try to avoid putting unnecessary hindrances in our congregation's way. The art is to preach what people may not want to hear in such a way that, in fact, they can.

One way to unify a congregation across its great diversity is through narrative. A good story, real or fictional, can touch the universal experiences that lie beneath our many differences. As Frederick Buechner wrote in his memoir, *The Sacred Journey*, "The story of any one of us is in some measure the story of us all." Buechner likens reading a memoir to looking through someone else's photograph album. "What holds you, if nothing else, is the possibility that somewhere among all those shots of people you never knew, you may come across someone you recognize. You may even catch a glimpse of yourself."[2] Listening to a good story told well has the same effect. All hear the experiences of another filtered through their own lives, reflecting on the other's struggles or triumphs in light of their own.

Once I was to preach on biblical texts exhorting generosity from the book of Deuteronomy.

> *If there is among you anyone in need, a member of your community, in any of the towns within the land that the Lord your God is giving you, do not be hard-hearted or tight-fisted toward your neighbor. You should rather open your hand, willing lending enough to meet the need.* — Deuteronomy 15:7-8

Knowing that many in the congregation believe in the virtues of generosity and that few would argue on the need for us as a society to be more generous, I decided to take a personal approach, reflecting out loud on the things that keep me from acting as generously as I would like:

> *I don't like it when I become hard-hearted or tight-fisted in response to someone in need, but I confess that, at times, I am. It's painful to acknowledge how closed my hands and heart can be, in direct contrast to the great teachings of our faith and the example of Jesus.*

43

What keeps me hard-hearted and tight-fisted even when I don't want to be? What holds my hands clenched when I would rather open them with unbridled generosity? Many things, I suppose, more than I will ever know. But I do know some of the demons that hinder me. They are: feeling overwhelmed and overextended; feeling anxious about my own needs and worrying about not having enough; and feeling empty and devoid of the love I am asked to offer others.

I then expanded on each feeling and what I have learned about God's grace coming to me in the midst of them.

It was a sermon about learning how to receive God's love in order to be able to give. I wanted those listening to experience something of the love that God asks us to share. The message came to me first, as I acknowledged my own limitations before God. Given what I knew of the congregation, I decided to speak personally, in order that they, listening to my struggles, might consider what holds them back from living as generously as God desires. I wanted them to know that God loves them in their struggles, too.

Thinking and praying about particular people throughout the week is essential when preparing a sermon. If I know someone struggling with grief, facing an important decision, or contemplating a life-changing adventure, I imagine what that person will hear or needs to hear, in my sermon. I don't mention specifics from the pulpit; I simply speak with an awareness that heightens my sensitivity. Likewise, if I am aware of tension in a family or conflict within the community, I speak carefully, knowing that all sides will be listening, at least in part, through the filter of that experience. Even in the absence of obvious disagreement, I assume that people will hear the message differently, according to what they bring from their own circumstances and beliefs.

Maintaining an awareness of differences helps us as preachers to think broadly, beyond our own opinion. Such awareness is particularly important when preaching on sensitive topics. The scriptures don't allow us to avoid them. Each week has the potential to offend or hurt someone. Our task is to engage delicate matters with compassion and awareness of how easily we can trigger anxiety, guilt, or anger in those listening.

One Sunday it was my task to preach on the story of the rich, young man whom Jesus told to sell all that he had, give it to the poor, and follow him (Mark 10:17-27). The gospel text for the previous week had been Jesus' teaching against divorce (Mark 10:2-10). The preacher that Sunday had offered a sincere, straightforward interpretation of the text, grounded in his experience as a happily married man and high school teacher who knew well the damaging effects of divorce on children. It was a fine sermon, yet preached with little pastoral sensitivity to those listening. Without realizing it, he touched a nerve. Many who had been divorced felt judged by someone who had no appreciation of their experience. It was my task to follow him in the pulpit and speak about yet another sensitive topic — money.

I knew that people were still thinking and talking about the previous sermon and wondered what I might say in response to it. Because I believe that one function of preaching is to help people think about important matters even if when those who hear disagree with the views expressed from the pulpit, I wanted to stand alongside the previous preacher. Some in the congregation were hurt, and I felt a pastoral responsibility to them, as well.

My goal was to honor both the previous sermon and the wide range of reaction to it. I began:

> *How we hear Jesus' teachings about money, or any other sensitive matter, depends in large measure on where we stand. It's one thing to hear Jesus condemn the rich man if we have little money; it's quite another should we have a lot. It's one thing to hear Jesus tell us to sell all we have when we have few family obligations and little need for material security; it's quite another when others are depending upon us for their well being. Thinking back to last week's gospel, it's one thing to hear Jesus' words on divorce when we are in a healthy marriage; it's quite another if our relationship is unraveling or ended, or, for that matter, if we've never been married. How we hear Jesus' words as recorded*

in scripture, and how we hear Jesus speaking to us through them, depends upon the unique prism of our life experience. And Jesus would have it no other way.

From there I went on to describe the subjectivity of human experience: how some feel wealthy when they have sufficient money to the pay the bills and others feel poor if they can't spend summers in Europe. I spoke of how marriage can be a channel of grace for some and a prison of unhappiness for others. I emphasized Jesus' desire to set us free from our destructive choices and debilitating guilt. My main message to the congregation, however, was inspired by the first sentence of the gospel passage: "We speak of what we know and testify to what we have seen." We all experience life differently and hear the gospel according to what we have known. God meets us where we are.

Preachers fortunate enough to occupy the same pulpit for years have a distinct advantage in knowing our congregations. Preaching over time has the feel of a sustained conversation with room for interaction and response from a congregation that knows its preacher well and, indeed, helps inform the preacher's words.

It is possible, however, to preach well to a community of strangers, as the new preacher, guest in another church, or keynote speaker at a community gathering. Such preaching requires particular care in preparation, and intentional effort at relationship building, beyond platitudes and superficial greetings. Whenever I am asked to speak outside of the congregation I serve, I start by listing all that I know about the people I will address. I try to learn as much as I can about them and think of them as I prepare. My first task from the pulpit, with my words and presence, is to make a personal connection.

I was once asked to preach at our diocesan convention, the yearly gathering of clergy and lay representatives from every congregation in the state. I had been in the diocese for less than two years and knew almost no one outside my own congregation. Yet I knew some things about those gathered for the convention. I knew that there would be a wide range of congregational and life experience among them, most with a long history to a place where I was still a newcomer. I suspected that many would be wondering why I was asked to preach, particularly among the other clergy, some who may have wanted the honor themselves. I knew that all would all be tired after a long weekend and ready to go home. I would have to work quickly to establish a personal connection to them, so they could hear the message I was to preach.

> *My friends, I am a newcomer in your midst, having served the good parish of St. John's in Minneapolis for just under eighteen months. On behalf of all who have been strangers here, I thank you for your warmth of welcome and generosity in allowing us to take a place in the legacy and ministry of the Diocese of Minnesota. It is a great privilege. I am one of the fortunate women for whom the process of ordination was relatively un-encumbered, and I give thanks to God for all of you who have toiled, often at great cost, so that our church might more fully reflect the love of God. Clearly we have much work yet before us, but I am profoundly grateful for how far we have come. With you and our bishop, I am willing to take up the cross for those who come after us.*
>
> *I would also like to acknowledge those of you who are called and willing to serve on the edges of our church, taking your place among the poor, the young and the old, the institutionalized, disenfranchised, and isolated. The personal cost of such ministry, both lay and ordained is very high, and we who work where life is gentler too often forget that. Thank you for all that you do in our name.*

I wanted each person listening to know that I valued their ministry and considered myself privileged to be among them. With that initial connection of respect and gratitude, I then told a joke to lighten the mood. Then I could preach, confident that the congregation would listen to what I had to say.

Another time I was invited to preach at a seminary congregation of students preparing for ministry and their professors. While I knew none of them personally, I shared with them the vocation of ministry. I came to them as a practitioner in the field for which they were being prepared, and I chose to speak to them as colleagues. The text for my sermon was from the book of Deuteronomy, in which God speaks of the need for prophets to speak words of truth and the harsh implications for those who are called but do not speak what God would have them say (Deuteronomy 18:15-20). I began, not with words of gratitude for being their preacher, but with a frank description of the vocation we shared:

> *The prophetic task is fraught with peril, from without and within. We who are called to leadership of any kind in Christ's church need to have our wits about us as we contemplate this particular dimension of our vocation. The first thing to say about it is that it is nonnegotiable. Having dedicated ourselves to the study of scripture, we know that from the beginning of our spiritual tradition God has raised up imperfect human beings like you and me to speak truth on God's behalf. "I will raise up for them a prophet like you," the Lord said to Moses, "from among their own people. I will put my word in the mouth of the prophet."*

With the tone established as one colleague speaking to others, I could preach about the power and peril of prophetic ministry.

In the pulpit we stand at the crossroads between our own relationship to God and our relationship to the congregation, and we speak to one about the other. There is also the mystery of preaching, whenever our reach is beyond us, somehow, into that mystical relationship between God and the congregation. For a brief, wondrous moment we are the channel through which God speaks to the people gathered, both individually and collectively. The power of that connection lies not in what we say, but how God speaks through our words. There are times, as every preacher knows, when what people hear is not what we say, as if the Holy Spirit intervenes and allows the precise message to reach particular ears. We need not understand this mystery of grace. Yet we are called to participate in it as one of the great privileges of ministry.

Preaching therefore deserves not only our best preparation but also humility, gratitude, and awareness of God's abiding love for all those listening to our words.

---

1. Fred B. Craddock, *Preaching* (Nashville: Abingdon Press, 1985), p. 88.

2. Frederick Buechner, *The Sacred Journey* (San Francisco: Harper & Row, 1982), p. 6.

Creating Community
Out Of A Crowd

While some dimensions of sermon preparation are personal and all hear a sermon from the perspective of their individual lives, preaching is, nonetheless, a social phenomenon. Preachers cannot preach to one person alone. A sermon requires the energy and spirit of a community gathered. There are social implications of a sermon that transcend what an individual might personally gain from it, precisely because the message is heard in community. Preaching is intended to move a community forward; indeed, to take a disorganized crowd and out of it make the people of God.

Jesus preached to groups of people. He spoke on several levels at once, affecting his listeners individually and in relationship to one another. He preached to the disciples with whom he shared life and ministry, creating a close-knit community among them. He preached to the crowds who hungered for healing and forgiveness. Jesus created community wherever he went, assuring those on the edges of human society that they belonged in the family of God. From his life, we know that one function of our preaching is to help create and sustain community.

We face several challenges here. The first is individualism, the cultural bias that encourages Americans to think of faith as something personal and private. While most people want meaningful relationships and authentic community, we aren't practiced in the values and skills that sustaining community requires. We choose our affiliations according to individual preference, and we feel perfectly justified leaving any community that doesn't meet our individual needs. There is value in such freedom, but it also works against what relationships need to thrive — perseverance, the willingness to work through conflict, and to compromise for the good of the whole.

A second challenge we face is the relatively low priority attending worship has become. Many who attend churches today see their faith commitment as one of many, and they wear it lightly in relationship to other priorities. Thus preachers must find ways to articulate a vision that speaks to people's desire for meaning and enhances their appreciation for what community provides. Gone are the assumptions of responsibility and duty that may have spoken to previous generations. It's our task to help our listeners go deeper in their understanding of what it means to live the Christian life and recognize the noble spiritual impulses that lie beneath superficial preoccupations and desires.

Preachers must also contend with the powerful affects of mass media, technologically based entertainment, and consumerism. These forces promote pseudo-community. They create the *feelings* of community without the personal commitment and sacrifice that community demands. As preachers we have the challenging task of learning to distinguish between the technologies of popular culture that are of great use to us and the cultural messages that are antithetical to the gospel. Similarly, we must draw upon the power of artistic expression throughout popular culture without losing sight of the eternal truths entrusted to us.

Christian community requires effort to nurture and sustain. For many attending our churches, it takes time to understand the importance of community and allow it to take root in their lives. Part of a preacher's task is to highlight and enhance the experience of the grace and love in a life shared with others. Such a task cannot be accomplished in one sermon but requires slow, steady attention, as an undercurrent beneath every spoken word.

I try to instill positive *esprit de corps* from the pulpit, based on gratitude for the treasure of Christian community entrusted to us. I take every occasion to emphasize the power and potential of our common life. Rarely is this the entire focus of the sermon, but it is often an important minor theme that helps strengthen the congregation's sense of identity and purpose.

Once, when preaching on the spirit of generosity from the gospel text, "For where your treasure is, there your heart will be also," I included an aside about giving to the church. It wasn't a stewardship sermon, and its primary message lay elsewhere. But the sermon provided an opportunity to highlight the values of community:

Most people give to the church, and I include myself here, with mixed motives in varying proportions: generosity, a sense of duty, and guilt. It's true that our financial gifts help pay the electric bills, both here and at my house. They provide hospitality for us and for others we may never meet, help pay for music and educational materials, and go beyond this community in countless ways. In short, our financial gifts help sustain the mission to which we are all committed. But they do not define us. What defines us as a community of God are those moments of abundance and generosity that we share, when we gather at celebrations of joy and sorrow. We share of ourselves so that others may live more fully, receive the lavish gifts of others, and take the time to care for one another.

Whenever we gather, we bring our bits and pieces, our anxieties and certainties. Out of all that bringing and all that we are, God creates a community of abundance, from which we can all receive and out of which we are moved to give more. We have our anxious moments as a community as well, but real as they are, they never have the final word. Such is the wonder and mystery of love. There is plenty to go around — more than enough, more than we can hold. Grace pours out of us like an overflowing cup. We cannot help but share it, and in the sharing we gain even more. (Proper 14, Year C, August 13, 1995)

Baptisms are wonderful occasions to speak on behalf of the community, calling it to its higher purpose, instilling a sense of pride and commitment. They provide steady reminders of who God calls us to become:

Seven children are to be baptized today. Each has already had the momentous experience of being born. Each faces great adventure and learning in the days and years ahead, and they will learn many things stepping out to greet the life God has given them. Our task this morning is to thank God for these children, and by their example and presence, remind ourselves that all

53

*that is worth knowing is learned by stepping out, tak-
ing risks, and reaching toward the God who reaches
toward us. We welcome them on the journey we ourselves walk, holding for them the questions we ourselves
ask, in the community of believers who seek knowledge
born of adventure and truth.* (Trinity Sunday, Year B,
June 15, 2003)

The point is not to be overly explicit on the theme of community,
but to touch it lightly and build, over time, a growing appreciation
for what it means to belong to the body of Christ.

Sometimes it's helpful to highlight the imperfections and
struggles of community life, honestly acknowledging the inevitable conflicts and disappointments that are part of any congregation. Again, this is best accomplished in small doses over time,
rather than leaving the task to those unhappy occasions when a
larger, more obvious struggle has surfaced. In preaching a sermon
on forgiveness, for example, I concluded with the following words:

*If forgiveness of any kind, in any way, is a struggle for
you, then you're in the right place. We're all struggling here. Just because it's the core value of our faith
doesn't mean that forgiveness is easy for us. It isn't.
This is the place we come to practice being open to the
gift of forgiveness.*

*One thing about Christian community: it affords
lots of opportunity to practice forgiveness, as does every other relationship of our lives. And that's a good
thing. Practicing forgiveness is what makes us Christians, followers of the one who lived and died and rose
again so that all might know the compassionate forgiveness of God.* (Proper 19, Year A, September 11,
2005)

My hope was to equip the congregation to deal with conflict and
gently speak to those easily disappointed by human failings. Preaching can thus help build the resilience and perseverance essential to
community life.

Preaching community with a light touch, as part of nearly every sermon, prepares the congregation to hear the occasional sermon that is almost exclusively focused on the community itself. In my experience, these sermons are event-driven: on the Sunday of the annual parish meeting, for example, when important congregational issues are addressed; or during the season of stewardship, when the church's need for money must be placed into a larger context of its ministry and vision; or when something has happened to affect the community as a whole.

Early one morning in the spring of 1997, a mechanical fire engulfed our church building. It began in the kitchen and quickly spread to the parish hall, office wing, and nursery school. While the main sanctuary was spared, the fire destroyed virtually every other part of the church.

The first Sunday after the fire I began my sermon by describing the relief efforts taking place in Grand Forks, North Dakota, a city four hours from Minneapolis that had been devastated by flood and fire that spring, and the care volunteers there had taken to salvage heirlooms, Christmas decorations, and photographs for the families who had lost their homes. I then described how the families of children in our church's daycare center wanted to sort through the rubble to find personal items — a favorite toy, a blanket, or artwork completed the day before. We weren't supposed to let them in, but we did anyway. Who could deny them the importance of those things?

As Christians, we believe in a sacramental world, which means that we recognize and experience the grace of God mediated through material things. So it hurts us when places of familiarity and routine goodness are destroyed.

On the other hand, these things are only signs, only symbols holding all the mysteries that cannot be seen, such as grace, compassion, mercy, commitment, and constancy. A kitchen matters less than the people who gather in it. A church is not a building but the community it houses. Were this whole building destroyed, as the people of Grand Forks could tell us, we would still be a community and still be a church. A fire that destroys a building serves to remind us of what really matters — the people in and around us, the relationships we share, and through them, the love of God we have known. (Trinity Sunday, Year B, May 25, 1997)

A crisis within the community can serve to remind us of the treasure we share.

On more ceremonial occasions, it is the preacher's task to cast a vision for the community, to define its ministry in bold and dramatic terms. Every year on the occasion of the congregation's annual meeting, I preach on our mission and the concrete possibilities for the coming year. Some years I have more clarity than others. I try not to articulate more vision than I have or speak cavalierly about all the things we might do. But with whatever pieces of insight I have discerned or gathered, my task on that day is to be the vision bearer for the community.

One year I cast our vision both forward and back, showing slides of photographs from our past that underscored the courageous, faithful witness of our forebears, and then looking toward the future, with specific proposals for the building up of our community, hospitality, faith formation, and public witness.

There is much for us to consider, talk over, and pray about together. This is an important moment. Who can know for certain what the future holds? We do know that God is infinitely patient, and that nothing of significance happens quickly. But I hope that we don't drag our feet now. I hope that one day our children's children will say of us, "They were the courageous ones. They were hopeful, adventuresome, bold, and generous. They were willing to risk for others' sake, and for us."

I concluded, as I do every year on annual meeting Sunday, inviting the congregation to read aloud our mission statement.

With sermons focused almost exclusively on the community itself, it's important to include other, more personal themes. Not everyone will have the same relationship to the community, and all need a word to take back with them into their lives and the world. Other themes allow others less connected to our community's ministry to find themselves in the sermon and receive something from it.

One year I began an annual meeting sermon reflecting on what it means to have a relationship with God:

> *I wonder if having a relationship with God is easier than we imagine. Maybe what Jesus said in his Sermon on the Mount is true: that we are, simply and completely, blessed — blessed in our poverty, our grief, and our hunger. In turn, we are a blessing whenever we strive, despite our imperfection, to be merciful, peacemakers, and agents of justice.*
>
> *What if we don't have to say a million prayers, grovel on our knees, or give away all that we have? What if what Micah said thousands of years ago is true? "You already know," he told them, "God has already told you that he requires but three things: that you do justice, love kindness, and walk humbly with your God."*

From those broader themes of spiritual life, I then described how for some people the desire to have a relationship with God draws them into Christian community, and from there, I moved into the vision of our particular congregation. My goal was to create space for everyone listening to consider their own relationship with God and to provide those of us within the community a broader perspective of the church's purpose. Such perspective helps prepare us for the times when God's word has a truly prophetic role — one that asks us to examine our society and its values in light of the gospel and what God would have us to do and be in the world.

Public Life And Prophetic Call

Preaching is a personal experience, grounded in our own relationship with God. Preaching is informed by our relationship to the people gathered, as we speak to those we know and love in our congregations. Preaching helps create a community out of a crowd, uniting strangers in a common journey of faith. But preaching is also a public event — public speech offered in the context of public worship. In many congregations, particularly those small enough for people to relate to one another as friends and family, we can easily lose sight of the public dimension of preaching. Yet, as those called to speak God's word, we speak not only to the congregation, but also to the culture and society to which we belong.

Standing in the pulpit, we take our place in the line of prophets who spoke in God's name with a message of communal judgment and collective hope. Preaching in the name of Jesus, we witness to his love and promise of reconciliation. We call those gathered in Christ's name to accept the higher purpose and calling of their lives — to help create a world of beauty, justice, and peace.

Jesus preached to the religious leaders of his day with words full of prophetic passion. We share in Jesus' ministry, as we care for the body of Christ and witness beyond it. Simply stated, social and prophetic preaching is a nonnegotiable dimension of our vocation.

When preaching prophetic sermons, we come up against our society's ambivalence about the role of religious leadership in public life. There is a strong feeling among many that preachers should refrain from addressing political issues from the pulpit. "I don't want to think about politics when I come to church," people have told me. "Church is the one place I can find respite from the mean-spiritedness of the world." Others don't know how to navigate their relationship to me when we disagree on public matters. "How can I come to you as my priest when I am so angered by what you said the previous Sunday?" one person asked. Still others expect me to preach on politics more often than I do. "Why aren't you saying more against the war?" they complained during the months leading up to the invasion of Iraq in 2003.

Whenever we speak to the political and social issues of the day, reactions can be intense, both positive and negative. A negative response is warranted whenever we enter the public arena cavalierly or with a narrowly focused agenda. Yet it could be that we simply touch a nerve for someone by challenging, consciously or otherwise, his or her worldview. In the sermon that I preached after Paul Wellstone's death, I made a statement in critique of our current state leadership, saying that we needed a public vision from our elected officials beyond that of not raising taxes. Three months later, a member of the congregation repeated that sentence back to me in a private conversation, saying that nothing had infuriated him more. While I believe what I said, his reaction gave me pause. For what he remembered with such emotion was not the point of my sermon, but one sentence I added as an afterthought, knowing that it would please the majority of the congregation listening.

Easy praise for public preaching is also dangerous, should we only confirm our listeners' social biases with our words. As law professor Stephen Carter cautioned in his book, *The Culture of Disbelief*, beware if Jesus always agrees with our political opinions. Chances are that instead of searching the scriptures to learn more about Christ and his claim on our lives, we have already decided what path we will intend to take and then look for evidence in scripture that God agrees.[1] If our preaching only confirms what most in our congregation believe or if it focuses only on the actions of others, we have failed in our prophetic task.

Prophetic preaching requires us to speak the truth that others know but cannot face. It involves shedding light on what we would all prefer to push outside the realm of consciousness and responsibility. The temptation of preaching prophetically is twofold: either to preach what our congregations want to hear, typically prophetic truths directed at *other* people; or to address those who see the world differently, presuming to speak for God, yet without love. The first temptation can lead to collective spiritual smugness; the second is simply arrogance. In the words of Israeli poet Yehuda Amichai, "From the place we are right flowers never grow in the spring. The place where we are right is hard and trampled like a yard." We do the gospel no service by speaking from self-righteous certainty. The biblical prophets took no pleasure in their words of judgment. They stood with their people under the judgment they proclaim out of love and in hope for a better day.

My approach is to speak of public concerns often, and in small doses. Occasionally I'll preach a strictly prophetic or community-focused sermon, but those occasions are rare, and I always include some message also directed at individual life and faith. In other words, I try to preach on several levels at once: speaking personally, for myself and others; addressing congregational issues; and touching upon matters of public concern and our responsibilities in society. I cannot give equal weight to each dimension in every sermon, but I try to anticipate how members of the congregation will hear the gospel message in light of their own lives, as well as listen for what God's word has to say for us as a people.

The sermon I cited earlier based on the text from Leviticus, "You shall not reap to the very edges of your field," was essentially about transgressing boundaries. I began with a personal confession: "Whatever it looks like to be faithful to this commandment, I'm certain that I'm not very good at it." I then moved to prophetic reflection:

> *In ancient Israel, commandments like this one resulted in enlightened social policy — one that gave the poor and landless a means of survival with a modicum of dignity. They had a place. It was their right to harvest to the edges of the fields that did not belong to them. They were entitled to the fallen grapes. It wasn't charity to leave the edges and the last grapes on the vine. It was a way for the community to define itself as one that provided for all its members, that left no one out, not even aliens. That was very important, for you see, the Israelites were once aliens in the land of Egypt.*
>
> *What would it look like for us not to reap to the edges of our field or gather the last grapes of our vineyard? Currently there is a tremendous housing shortage for workers of modest income — the people who care for our children, build our roads, and process our*

foods. Many of the people upon whose labors our lives depend cannot afford to live in our communities. Why is that? Perhaps because we as a society tend to harvest to the very edge of our fields. We take the last grapes for ourselves, so that there is nothing to spare. (Easter 5, Year C, May 13, 2001)

Throughout the sermon I continued a balanced reflection of the ways we as individuals and as a society transgress boundaries. I used the example of time. ("Think what it feels like when every minute of the day is spoken for, when your calendar is completely filled.") I used examples of personal resources and the assumptions we make about one another. That way, everyone listening could reflect on their lives in light of God's teachings, as well as consider the kind of society God would have us create. The feeling of judgment is softened when we speak as people alongside our listeners, standing under the same prophetic word of God.

There are times, of course, when events of the larger community or the world break in and demand our attention. We would be remiss not to address the prophetic truths suggested or revealed in times of crisis, yet the task of prophetic preaching is most perilous here. All can bring to mind the embarrassing examples of preachers who in times of national disaster spoke cavalierly of God's judgment, revealing little more than their own prejudices. While it is tempting to avoid prophetic risks from the pulpit, for fear of causing conflict or sounding foolish, our vocation demands otherwise. God calls us to proclaim truth in difficult times.

The events of recent years have tested the prophetic sensibilities of every preacher. On seemingly innocent mornings, we've awakened to news of terrorist attacks, both in the United States and abroad. We've endured years of an ambiguous, inconclusive, and costly war. There are constant reports of violence and natural disasters throughout the world. In one year alone, we experienced untold human devastation caused by the tsunami in Southeast Asia, hurricanes Katrina and Rita in the United States, and the earthquake of Pakistan. How does one speak on the Sunday after such cataclysmic events?

I generally begin by making a human connection to whatever has happened to rock our world, acknowledging how difficult it can be to comprehend the magnitude of such events. Two weeks after the World Trade Center attacks in September 2001, I simply stated that whenever we are faced with something we've never experienced before, one of the things we lose is our point of reference. We simply don't have the means to interpret what has happened or predict what's coming next. On the Sunday after the bombing of the London transit system in July 2005, I began by associating the deep dismay felt throughout London that the suicide bombers were British citizens to the American experience ten years earlier when we learned that US citizens bombed the Federal Building in Oklahoma City.

The Sunday after Hurricane Katrina, I began by referencing William Styron's novel, *Sophie's Choice*, where the main character realized, to his horror, that during his idyllic childhood the woman he now loved had experienced the worst cruelties of the Holocaust.

> *How could it be, he wondered, that at the exact same moment two people would experience the world so differently — one in a living hell while the other was surrounded by gentle blessings?*
>
> *No doubt we've all asked our own version of that question this week, as we've basked in the beauty of Minnesota in late summer. For as we've had the privilege of tending to our own lives, downstream on the Mississippi River thousands have had unimaginable destruction, degradation, and death visited upon them. How can it be?*

The objective in all three instances was the same: to establish a relationship, a starting point grounded in our own experience from which to begin the task of preaching.

The next step in prophetic preaching is to describe in simple and stark language the reality before us. There is little need for elaboration in a society overrun by television images and round-the-clock commentary. This is simply a gentle reminder of what has happened. After September 11, I summed up the tragedy in a paragraph:

> *This is a war, the president has told us, but unless a foreign government is implicated, the metaphor of war, as one writer noted, "may ascribe to the perpetrators a dignity they do not merit." It is a tragedy, yet of a proportion not fully comprehended, with personal, economic, and military reverberations still to be felt. We simply don't know how to continue our lives as our leaders have asked us to do. Then there is the toll of grief. We're exhausted at the end of each day from the weight of sorrow resting on our soldiers.* (September 23, 2001)

The point is to bring events to mind in vivid, yet open-ended language, so that each person can do the important work of taking in what has happened.

The next and most important task in prophetic preaching is also deeply pastoral: to remind people of the great spiritual resources we have to draw upon in times of crisis.

The Christian faith is at its best in times of adversity, something easily forgotten or never learned until life gets hard. Our sacred scriptures can give us courage, perspective, and the capacity to endure. Our history is full of examples of ordinary people finding what they need to face the crises of their day. After September 11, I preached from the perspective of history, citing the best speeches from earlier times of adversity in our country. I drew from the richness of the Bible, particularly the Hebrew scriptures. In the rabbinic tradition, only three books of the scriptures are to be read in times of grief: Lamentations, Job, and Jeremiah. The rest are set aside. So I read from those texts: "For the hurt of my poor people I am hurt, I mourn, and dismay has taken hold of me. Is there no balm in Gilead? Is there no physician here?"

Where is God when calamity strikes? While human beings have asked that question from the beginning of time, it is always a new question when we ask it in the face of immediate suffering. And we must ask it from the pulpit. We ask for ourselves and for all those who stumble into church looking for some kind of answer.

Initially, the answer is always one of silence: "My God, my God, why have you forsaken me?" We would be dishonest if we did not acknowledge the devastating silence. But there is also the mystery of presence — God's presence with us in the midst of all that has happened.

To speak of God's presence and comfort in times of trial is as true to prophetic speech as is speaking the harder truths of judgment. "Comfort, comfort my people," God instructed the prophet Isaiah in his nations' darkest hour and through those words to us. The grace of God is real, able to see us through the hardest things.

Another dimension of prophetic preaching can highlight the depth and complexity of our faith tradition in response the great mysteries of human suffering and the reality of evil in our world. There are no easy explanations, and we serve our congregations well by highlighting the wide range of insight and response available to us in scripture.

On the Sunday after the London transit bombings in July 2005, the appointed gospel text was the parable of the weeds among wheat (Matthew 13:24-30). Its message is one of tolerance, as the master instructs his servants to allow the weeds and wheat to grow alongside each other until the harvest, when God alone will collect the wheat and cast the weeds into the fire. The parable provided a rich and provocative lens through which to consider the reality of evil. "The terrorists are not strangers or foreigners," one official of the European Union said. "They are insiders, well integrated inside the country." Yet this parable was not Jesus' only word on the reality of evil, and it felt important to acknowledge the breadth of his teaching.

> *Before delving into the parable's obvious call for tolerance and patience, let me point out that it is not Jesus' only word on dealing with sin and evil. In other passages from this same gospel, Jesus can be quite harsh. He talks a lot about final judgment, warning that there will be severe consequences for those who reject God.*
>
> *In one passage, Jesus suggests a strict protocol of escalating confrontation when dealing with an unrepentant sinner in the church, and when speaking to*

65

church leaders, he is particularly firm: "If your hand
causes you to sin," he warns, "cut it off; if your eye
causes you to sin; pluck it out; it is better for you to
lose one of your members than for your whole body to
go into hell" (Matthew 5:28-30).

At other times, however, in this same gospel, Jesus
speaks of lavish forgiveness. When Peter asks him how
many times he should forgive another, and suggest per-
haps as many as seven times, Jesus replies, "Not seven,
but seventy times seven" (Matthew 18:21). Forgiveness
and mercy are at the heart of the Sermon on the Mount:
"Turn the other cheek; walk the extra mile. Give not
only your shirt, but your coat as well" (Matthew 5).

My point is simply that Jesus' teachings are com-
plex and varied. He doesn't say the same thing over
and over; each situation calls for a particular response.
Sometimes Jesus speaks of accountability and judgment,
and at other times of mercy and forgiveness. In parables
like the one about the wheat and weeds, or of the sun
shining and rain falling on the just and the unjust, he is
an advocate of tolerance. Without minimizing the real-
ity of evil, he tells us that sometimes it is wise to exer-
cise restraint. Let the weeds grow alongside the wheat
until the proper time. Judgment belongs not to you, but
to God. (July 17, 2005)

I dedicated the rest of the sermon to the parable's wisdom of tolerance, set in the context of the breadth of Jesus' teaching.

The final task to prophetic preaching in response to a dramatic event is to touch, very lightly, upon the most difficult questions of judgment raised by such a calamity. In the face of shock
and suffering, it would be inappropriate to dwell heavily here for
long. But truth avoided only serves to raise anxiety. It is better and
more reassuring to gently speak truth. I ended my first post-Sep-
tember 11 sermon this way:

At some point we must come to terms with the origins
of hatred so strategically targeted at the symbols of our
prosperity and military power. When the president

raised the question, "Why do these people hate us?"
he answered by saying, "They hate our values and our
freedom." This is partially true: fundamentalists of all
faiths, not just Islam, share a deep disdain for many of
the positive values of modern society that we cherish,
which is all the more shocking when that disdain in a
small minority turns violent. But it is not the full truth,
and we deserve more. We deserve a deeper understand-
ing of our role in the Arab world and the impact of our
presence there.

We needn't be patronized with simplistic explana-
tions and patriotic slogans. We are capable of learning
why the seeds of discontent have been sown so suc-
cessfully against us. It is a big task, one that we weren't
prepared for, but we have the means to face it, and face
it we must, if we are to prevail in our effort to rid the
world of such crimes. (September 23, 2001)

The Sunday after Hurricane Katrina, I concluded my sermon, which had been primarily focused on how we could offer concrete aid and support for those affected by the floods, with a similarly gentle reminder of a difficult truth:

There is another way we will respond, in time, as part
of a national conversation about our priorities and
subsequent vulnerabilities as a country. This is a wake-
up call and an opportunity to bring the best of who we
are, as people of faith and as citizens, into public
conversation. It will be a conversation about what
national preparedness means, and what investment in
civic infrastructure requires. It will be, at long last, a
conversation about institutional racism and poverty in
this country. For that conversation, we must be strong,
clear, and ready to speak the truth God has entrusted
to us. (September 4, 2005)

Such reminders, however, are part of a larger, sustained conversation in preaching that speaks prophetic truths on a regular basis so that we are spiritually prepared for hardships and disasters when they strike.

67

Indeed, prophetic preaching is best accomplished over time, drawing upon the depth of scripture and reasoned, historical reflection to interpret our world in light of God's presence and word. As preachers, we should take every opportunity given to preach prophetically with a pastoral touch, so that all who hear know that we stand under the same prophetic judgment and rely the same prophetic comfort that we proclaim.

For lectionary preachers, there are numerous opportunities each year to delve into the prophetic literature of the Bible and to consider the prophetic ministry of Jesus, particularly in the season of Lent. There are also national holidays that lend themselves to a more civic-minded word from the pulpit, which I have found to be almost universally appreciated by those listening.

Years ago, as I prepared to preach on the Sunday before the first official Martin Luther King holiday, I read a collection of King's speeches and sermons. Deeply moved by his words, I simply stood in the pulpit that Sunday and read excerpts of his writings. I have done the same every year since on the Sunday prior to the Martin Luther King holiday. It is now a congregational event. Some years I have used the occasion to highlight some aspects of civil rights history, with a particular eye for the role of religion in the struggle for justice and the courageous examples of countless Americans who risked their lives for what they knew was right.

Most years I simply read King's words and allow their power to speak for themselves, seeking his words of counsel, acknowledgment of struggle, and testimony of faith and courage:

> *Never succumb to the temptation of becoming bitter.*
> *As you press on for justice, be sure to move with dignity*
> *and discipline, using only the weapon of love. Let no*
> *one pull you down so low as to hate.*
>
> *I believe that standing up for the truth of God is*
> *the greatest thing in the world. This is the end of life.*
> *The end of life is not to be happy. The end of life is not*
> *to achieve pleasure and avoid pain. The end of life is to*
> *do the will of God, come what may.*[2]
>
> *My personal trials have also taught me the value*
> *of unmerited suffering. As my sufferings mounted I soon*

*realized that there were two ways that I could respond
to my situation: either to react with bitterness or seek
to transform suffering into a creative force. I decided
to follow the latter course ... The suffering and agoniz-
ing moments through which I have passed over the last
few years have also drawn me closer to God. More than
ever before I am convinced of the reality of a personal
God.*[3]

The spiritual practice of preaching from King's life every January has made me an avid student of the Civil Rights Movement. It
has deepened the congregation's awareness and understanding of
the spiritual foundations of social change, and it has served as an
important corrective to our society's tendency to romanticize King.
More important, it has given us all the opportunity to hear, year
after year, the depth of his wisdom, spiritual courage, and faith.
Many have told me that it is a sermon they look forward to hearing
every year. It is one that I love to preach, although I feel the weight
of its judgment on my own life and ministry, seen through the lens
of King's clarity of social witness.

Indeed, with all prophetic sermons, there is a necessary discomfort, for we stand in the light of God's call to live as we believe, or, "to walk our talk." Here the connection between preaching and leadership is essential. For if we do not lead in ways that
help align our congregations' ministries to the prophetic truths we
preach, our words do more harm than good. But when we strive
for faithfulness in word and deed, we help shape communities of
justice and integrity. For all the inevitable tension that prophetic
preaching creates, it also instills a deep sense of pride throughout
the congregation. Most people want to belong to a community that
stands for something and strives to make the world a better place.
They want to be challenged and inspired. It is our task to speak
prophetic truth and lead our communities to the kind of action that
truth requires.

1. Stephen Carter, *The Culture of Disbelief* (New York: Anchor Books, 1994), p. 70.

2. Martin Luther King Jr., "The Most Durable Power (1958)" in *A Testament of Hope: The Essential Writings of Martin Luther King, Jr.*, James M. Washington, ed., (New York: HarperCollins Publishers, 1986), pp. 8-10.

3. *Ibid*, "Suffering and Faith (1960)," pp. 41-42.

The Sermon As Art

If we are to speak well, addressing the great issues of our time or the quiet concerns of our hearts, we must organize our thoughts into some coherent message. No matter the kind of sermon I feel inspired to preach, no matter the kind of week I've had to prepare, before I can stand before the congregation and say anything at all, I need to gather up the fragments and write. If I'm lucky, rubber meets pavement on Thursday afternoon. More than likely it will be Friday, or after a tough week, Saturday. The hour is late, the preparation process incomplete. I have what I have and don't have what I don't have. That is the time for spinning straw into gold.

I never know how I'm going to feel when I sit down to pull the pieces of a sermon together. My emotions can range from excitement to dread, energy to fatigue, gratitude to resentment. But feelings are largely irrelevant now; the task is clear. I've learned that there is no correlation between my feelings at the start of a sermon and its quality. So I try to be kind with myself, but also firm. It's time. Sit down. Sit down now.

I prefer to write at home. At church I am tempted with urgent and important work that must now be put aside. There are also tasks at home. The house is never cleaner than on the day I begin to write. I walk the dog, often. I do laundry. I tell the church administrator that I'm available to take phone calls at home. Yes, by all means, interrupt me. I'm working on a sermon, but I need diversion, too.

Distractions keep me sane while the relative quiet at home keeps me on task. I take phone calls, have a meeting, if necessary, and shop for groceries. Nonetheless, on the day when preparing to preach is my central task, I place my best energies there even as I tend to the frazzled edges of my life.

It helps if I begin by assembling the material gathered throughout the week with a light touch. I jot down how the scripture texts speak to me. I collect my thoughts about what I've read, heard, or seen. I think about what has happened to me personally, in the parish, and the larger world. I hold in my heart those who will gather

71

on Sunday and consider what I know of their lives. Most important, I set down what has held my attention throughout the week, the thought that I can't let go of, the story that demands telling.

Seasoned writers often encourage the rest of us not to fear the messiness of a first draft, and in preaching the same truth applies. Typically, I begin several steps away from even the messiest of first drafts with jumbled thoughts, streams of consciousness writing, and lists of things I want to remember. I start with pen to paper, because paper allows me greater freedom in the early stages. That's not true for everyone; my children and their peers never write anything on paper before turning on their computers. One's means of beginning matters less, however, than the beginning itself. In the words of the author Nora Gallagher, who taught me more about writing in a four-day seminar than I'd learned in a lifetime, this is the time to *generate material*. It's time to string pieces together in the first attempt of narration, telling the sermon's story.

I used to worry that I began my sermons not knowing how they would end. Now I know that's what good writing requires. How could I possibly know the ending as I start? Like other forms of creation, a sermon begins in chaos.

So I write pages of illegible script, working so fast that I can't keep up with my own thoughts. The progression of thought makes perfect sense to me as I'm writing, although later I often can't follow my line of reasoning or even read what I've written. Sometimes I go back and attempt to make sense of it. The initial writing serves a purpose that isn't always related to what eventually becomes the terrible first draft. But with the messiest writing behind me, I turn on the computer and begin again.

Rituals are important in writing, and I have several. I begin each sermon the same way. At the top left-hand corner of the page I write the word "Sermon," followed by the day of the liturgical calendar, such as 4 Lent, Year B. Below that I write the date the sermon will be preached. Then I write where I'll preach the sermon, most often the church where I am rector. Below the location, I write my name. Each line grounds me in a particular reality, reminding me what time it is, where and to whom I will preach, and who I am.

Then I type the scripture passage that serves as the sermon's inspiration. Later it may be helpful for anyone reading the sermon to know the biblical source, but as I type, the passage is for me. Taking time to write the scripture, pen to paper or keyboard to screen, calms my nerves and focuses my thoughts. It reminds me of Jesus. It also makes my work feel official. I am now writing a sermon.

I spend a lot of time, perhaps too much, crafting the opening sentence. But I need a place to begin. In journalism and literature the first sentence reveals the heart of a story, and I feel that a sermon's first sentence must do the same. In the pulpit, as in theater, there is great power in a strong opening line. If you get it right, the congregation will listen. If you miss, their thoughts will wander. But the right beginning is for my sake, too. The beginning that first comes to me I may well discard later, but no matter. I need something with which to take the plunge.

I've learned to begin with the best I've got, the strongest point, the most compelling story. Annie Dillard, in her wise book on writing, puts it this way:

> One of the few things I know about writing is this: spend
> it all, shoot it, play it, lose it all right away, every time.
> Do not hoard what seems good for a later place ... The
> impulse to save something good for a better place is
> the signal to spend it now.[1]

I start with my best, and then write in a style that feels more like compilation, stringing ideas in a sequence not yet clear.

Nora Gallagher likens the first draft to letter writing. She says to imagine that you are writing to an intelligent, attentive friend who wants to know how things are going. Let your mind flow from one idea to the next and write freely. As I write, a new thought may come. I have no idea if it fits into the sermon, but I follow it. If it turns out to be a dead-end, I'll take it out later. It may be the heart of a sermon I didn't realize I was writing. Experienced writers say to trust those impulses. The less you know about the story, or the sermon, as you begin, the better.

With nearly every sermon, I have a crisis of vocation. It usually comes sometime after I've written my first illegible thoughts, which made so much sense as I wrote them but now seem worthless, and before I finish my official first draft. The writing isn't going well, the pieces I've gathered don't seem to fit, or I'm tired. I realize that I don't want to be a priest anymore. I resent having to work on a beautiful Saturday afternoon. My family has learned to avoid me at such times. For the only thing that keeps me going is the dread of disappointing those who'll be in church the next day expecting to hear something worth the effort they made to be there.

At this juncture a strong work ethic is helpful. All preachers need a firm inner voice to cut through the self-pity and well-rehearsed whining in order to keep going when we don't want to. The poet, Robert Bly, speaks of having an inner warrior, which is exactly what I need on Saturday afternoon. We also need to give ourselves some room. If I can't think anymore, I take a walk or rest on the couch. If the pieces aren't fitting, I leave them for a while and see what I can make of them when I return. But I don't give up. There's something to figure out, a mystery to solve, a thread of ideas to pursue. After all, this is why the church pays me. I'm the one who is going to stand before everyone and speak on Sunday. I try not to panic.

Like most crises, the I-never-want-to-preach-another-sermon-in-my-life feeling passes. Something will happen to lift my mood, or even if it doesn't, I forge ahead. I come back to the sermon after an hour and realize that it wasn't as hopeless as I thought, or I see now how to fix it. I'll read an article in the newspaper or passage from a novel that very day that fits perfectly into what I'm trying to say. Someone will say something in passing or a thought occurs to me that forms the bridge between two previously disconnected ideas.

At some point, no matter how late in the day, I put the sermon aside. I've done as much as I can see to do, and I need to clear my brain in order to see the sermon later with fresh eyes. Sometimes walking away from a sermon feels like surrender. It doesn't seem like enough, but it's the best I have. Other times I feel nothing at all, except the physical need to move, to think about anything other than what I've written or failed to write. I've learned that this is precisely the right thing to do. Nora Gallagher explains why: "In the process of writing," she said, "you figure out what your material is. As you write, it happens. When you step away from your writing to do other things, your unconscious is still processing. When you return, it gives you a gift."

When I return late in the day on Saturday, after an evening out, or early Sunday morning, I focus on the sermon's core message and the best way to communicate it. Then the process of sermon writing becomes — dare I say it? — fun. I now have enough ideas to work with and some to discard. I play with the sermon's structure and hone its core message. If need be, I continue searching for material, but now with focus. Even if I'm still struggling to find a missing piece or organizational tool, the process has become energizing, even exhilarating.

In these final hours, the craft of sermon writing is foremost in my mind, and I bring all my critical skills to the task. How can I tighten the prose? Do the stories I tell serve the core message? If not, I take them out, even if I love them. Are there throwaway lines, sentences that I've included to cause a reaction but aren't necessary to the sermon? I take those out, too.

This is the kind of work that distinguishes many good sermons from a few great ones. For a congregation to be edified, it probably isn't necessary to work this hard right to the end. What we have to say before this last effort of review, critique, and careful editing is surely adequate for those with ears to hear to hear God's truth. The Spirit is generous and will work with whatever we offer. But the *art* of preaching requires fierce loyalty to the truth entrusted to us and the words with which to communicate it.

Early on Sunday, I review the sermon one more time with the fresh eyes of morning. Sometimes that last editing is significant; other times less so. Often I must stop because it's time. The work of preparation is over. The time has come to offer back what I've received.

---

1. Annie Dillard, *The Writing Life* (New York: HarperPerennial, 1989), p. 78.

The Gift Of A Sermon

Like many clergy, I preach first at 8 a.m. to a chapel congregation of less than twenty. The chapel is an intimate space; the pulpit is situated a short distance away from the first row of chairs. In this setting, preaching feels like conversation among friends, except in that moment, I'm doing all the speaking. Still, I try to honor the chapel's space and tone, speaking directly and gently to those gathered. No need for large projection skills here. A simple delivery works best.

The feedback from this first congregation is always generous and supportive. Yet as I preach, I listen for what seems to fit and what doesn't. While I almost always preach from a manuscript, I sometimes depart from it, and if I've done so here, I make note if the inclusion or omission is worth adding to the text for the later services. There isn't much time for revision at this point, but the revision process is still at work, as I take in the response of those who first hear the sermon and my own experience in preaching it.

I preach the same sermon in two later services: one for a high-energy, relaxed congregation full of children; the other, for a more quiet and reflective gathering in the context of formal liturgy. In such varied contexts, there is no doubt that preaching is a communal event, an exchange of ideas and energy. The words are virtually the same in each service, yet the mood and energy can greatly vary. Jokes that were showstoppers at one service might barely register a response at another. Parts of the sermon that one congregation hardly hears are more deeply taken in at another. In one service, I might preach over considerable noise; in another to deep silence.

Of all the training I received to prepare and deliver sermons, the most helpful skills in delivery I learned in theater. Liturgy, at its best, is an art form, a drama in which we all participate. While presiding at worship and preaching in the pulpit is not acting, there is a degree of theatrical detachment necessary to preside and preach well. We are fully ourselves in that moment, but also representative of something much bigger than us. We put on our robes, turn on the microphone, and attempt to lay aside all the stresses and preoccupations of our lives to focus on the task at hand. We give ourselves to our role as preacher — a messenger of God's word. In the pulpit we need to be able to read the congregation and respond, have access to all of one's emotions without being overrun by them, and focus on the message we are there to proclaim.

Delivery is important, and I work at the skills required to deliver a sermon well. Posture, projection, and timing all play a part in how a sermon is received. Preaching well requires that we find our own voice, but allow it to be another's voice at the same time, to craft our words while allowing them to be God's word to a particular congregation. I am who I am as I preach, and I speak plainly and even conversationally — to people, not *at* them. Yet there is also the danger of getting in the way of the sermon if I focus too much on my experience in preaching it. As I prepared to deliver my first sermon to the congregation that had raised me, the priest who had known me since childhood said, "Remember, you are not the essential one here. *God* is the one they have come to hear."

As preachers, we cannot judge our sermons from our experience of writing and delivering them. While there are times when we are preaching well and we know it, and other times when we aren't preaching well and know that, too, the simple fact that once we are preaching, the sermon no longer belongs to us but to God and to those listening. All preachers have had the experience (or soon will) of someone telling them that the sermon they were certain was the worst they had preached was, in fact, a vehicle of grace. More humbling, many of the sermons we considered brilliant touched no one at all. We never can tell and we never know for sure; such is the mystery and gift of preaching.

It takes a while to get a sermon out of my system once I've preached it. Sometimes on Sunday afternoons, I'll hear it in my head, often taking a part of its truth for myself at a deeper level or wishing I had had more time to think it through. Mostly, I'm grateful for the miracle of the loaves and fishes once more. By Monday morning, I've corrected mistakes, added the proper citations, and sent a written text to the church administrator, who makes copies for anyone who wants them. Then it's time to let the sermon go and begin again. Next Sunday's sermon is the one to think about.

A Year
Of Sermons

You Are Responsible For Your Rose

Comfort, O comfort my people, says your God. Speak tenderly to Jerusalem, and cry to her that she has served her term, that her penalty is paid, that she has received from the Lord's hand double for all her sins. A voice cries out: "In the wilderness prepare the way of the Lord, make straight in the desert a highway for our God. Every valley shall be lifted up, and every mountain and hill be made low; the uneven ground shall become level, and the rough places a plain. Then the glory of the Lord shall be revealed, and all people shall see it together, for the mouth of the Lord has spoken. A voice says, "Cry out!" And I said, "What shall I cry?" All people are grass, their constancy is like the flower of the field. The grass withers, the flower fades, when the breath of the Lord blows upon it; surely the people are grass. The grass withers, the flower fades; but the world of our God will stand forever. Get you up to a high mountain, O Zion, herald of good tidings; lift up your voice with strength, O Jerusalem, herald of good tidings, lift it up, do not fear; say to the cities of Judah, "Here is your God!" See, the Lord God comes with might, and his arm rules for him; his reward is with him, and his recompense before him. He will feed his flock like a shepherd; he will gather the lambs in his arms, and carry them in his bosom, and gently lead the mother sheep. — Isaiah 40:1-11*

The beginning of the good news of Jesus Christ, the Son of God. As it is written in the prophet Isaiah, "See, I am sending my messenger ahead of you, who will prepare your way; the voice of one crying out in the wilderness: 'Prepare the way of the Lord, make his paths straight.' "   — Mark 1:1-3

The Little Prince lay down and wept at the sight of 500 roses in a garden. You see, on the planet he ruled, he had a single rose who had told him that she was unique. Yet, here were 500 roses, just like her, in one garden. "She would be very much annoyed if she knew," he said to himself. "She would cough most dreadfully and pretend that she was dying, to avoid being laughed at. And I should be obliged to pretend that I was nursing her back to life." *I thought that I was rich*, he thought sadly, *with a flower unique in all the universe*. If she was but an ordinary rose, who, then, was he?

Then the Little Prince met a fox that taught him an important lesson about love. "To me," the fox said, "you are nothing more than a little boy who is just like 1,000 other little boys. I have no need of you. And you have no need of me. I am just a fox, like 100,000 other foxes. But if you tame me, then we shall need each other. To me, you will be unique in all the world, and I will be the same for you."

The Little Prince returned to the garden of 500 roses and realized that for all their beauty, he felt nothing for them. But he loved his rose far away on his tiny planet — the rose he watered and sheltered and cared for. "It is the time you have wasted for your rose that makes her so important," the fox told the Little Prince. "You are responsible for your rose."[1]

The Christian faith, in its entirety, rests on one spiritual proposition: When God chose to redeem the world, God did not send an army, or a committee, or a plan, but a person — one person. Jesus lived in a particular place and time. He was born of Mary. And through his one life we see the human face of God. We who call ourselves Christians are those who feel so drawn to his life that we seek to live our lives in light of his. Our gospel — our good news — is the story of his life.

The gospel begins: A voice cries out, "In the wilderness prepare the way of the Lord, make his paths straight." How are we to prepare? How, in other words, are we, as Christians, to live? It's a haunting question in a world that needs so much: What is our responsibility? Who or what, in this moment and time, is our rose?

Our first responsibility must always be for ourselves, for the lives with which we are uniquely entrusted. For no one else can live our lives for us, nor can we live another's life. While we will never understand the great mysteries of inequity and suffering, the randomness of fortune and disaster, we can choose our response to life, how we seek to live in our own skin, how we allow the grace of God in, enabling us to love, forgive, let go, and reach out in ways that we could never do on our own. We are responsible for our rose.

Our second realm of responsibility is within the tapestry of relationships of our immediate sphere of relationships of family, friends, and community. It is no small task to love well those closest to us and to own our part in the universal imperfection of relationships; no small task to seek the best in one another, and forgive the worst; no small task to do our part and more when life demands it. We are responsible for our rose.

The third realm of responsibility is our work in the world, our vocation and contribution to the greater good. Through work, we take our energies and gifts and offer them up and out, beyond us. The realm of vocation is perhaps the hardest to discern, because, of course, it changes over time. Sometimes our work will be related to what we do for a living, but not always. Sometimes we are rewarded and recognized for our work, but often we are not. Sometimes our work puts us right in the center of things, but more often than not we are on the sidelines, working on behalf of someone else. Think of John the Baptist: his entire life, passionately lived, was a prologue for Jesus' ministry. "There is one who is coming who is greater than I," he said. "I am not worthy to untie the thong of his sandals."

One thing we do know about our work: It has nothing to do with what we consume and everything to do with how we contribute, how we make the world a better place by our presence. Work helps us find our place and connects us to something bigger. The former Czech president, Vaclav Havel, said it this way: "By perceiving ourselves as part of the river, we take responsibility for the river as a whole." We are all responsible for our rose.

For the importance of each realm of our responsibilities, life rarely affords us the luxury of apportioning equal amounts of energy to them. More typical is for one area to take priority for a time, be it self, relationships, or vocation. As a young adult, I tried to talk myself out of the pain I felt inside by focusing all my energies on those who had life harder than I did. My college roommates dubbed me the champion for every underdog on the planet. I always tried to give away more than I had, until at last I crashed on the rocks of my own woundedness. It was then that a kind and wise person pointed out to me that self-sacrifice isn't worth much if you don't have a self to begin with. I realized that if I didn't tend to the gaping hole in my heart, I would be forever hindered in my efforts to love, a lesson I have learned dozens of times since. I am responsible for my rose. You are responsible for yours.

In a similar way, when life requires us to drop everything for the sake of one we love, there is no option, really, but to go. We might deny for a time the enormity of what is asked of us and hold onto other commitments we care about but such efforts are futile. I remember when one in our family was rushed to the hospital for emergency surgery; how I tried to bring into the waiting room with me all of my work in preparation for the weekend. I had a sermon to write, a wedding to prepare for, and several meetings to plan. The extent of the crisis had clearly not yet sunk in, and I was trying to fit it in with my other responsibilities. It took the reality check of a friend, who gently but firmly told me that my priorities had shifted, and I wasn't going into work that weekend. When someone in our immediate circle needs us, we belong there. We are responsible for our rose.

Yet, there are also times when our work requires that kind of singular focus and energy, for creativity's sake, or to accomplish whatever it is that we feel called to. When work demands it, the other realms of family and self suffer for a time. It's a dangerous way to live indefinitely, but sometimes it's necessary, for the sake of a greater good. Years ago, the *New York Times* ran a story about a group of scientists at the National Institute of Health who realized that they were nearing a breakthrough in some treatment for a rare form of leukemia. Driven by the hope of new treatment, they worked around the clock for weeks, missing their children's soccer games and piano recitals so that someone else might live to see their own children play.

Think of the people you admire, in any field, whose memoirs and biographies you read. They are ones, generally, who dedicate significant portions of their lives to their work, who don't imagine they can transform the world in a forty-hour week, who take their vocations so deeply to heart that, in the end, they embody the essence of that work for us. Consider, again, John the Baptist. He wasn't exactly a balanced person. He felt responsible for his rose.

I first read the story of the Little Prince when I was a new parent, still struggling with the enormous shifting of energy and life priorities that parenting required. I was both comforted and challenged by the image of the rose. I was comforted in that I knew, with unmistakable clarity where my responsibility lay. And I was challenged, because I realized that if I didn't rise to this, if I couldn't love this one child, then all my efforts to love and to give in other realms would mean nothing.

Now, whenever my life calls me to focused effort or love of any kind; when I catch myself worrying about the time I am wasting or other contributions I'm not making because of that focus, I think of the rose. What we don't realize until we give ourselves to the singularity of love, of course, is that it stretches our hearts, not diminishes them. It makes us bigger inside, not smaller. We grow deeper in our capacities to love. The love itself, singularly and intensely offered, expands and goes forth from us. When we tend to ourselves, there is more of us to share or give away someday. When we tend to our immediate sphere of relationships, we build a foundation of compassion and health that reaches across generations. When we focus on our work, with all our creativity and best effort, we share in God's redeeming of the world.

I also think of the Little Prince every year as Christmas approaches, because of the one rose. "Lo, how a rose e'er blooming," we will sing on Christmas Eve. "It came a blossom bright, amid the cold of winter, when half spent was the night."[2] There is a haunting singularity about our faith, focused on one person, one baby born long ago. Yet it is the power and presence of that one life, living in us, that holds the promise of the reconciliation, redemption, and peace. It may not feel like enough but it is God's way, in and through us. Jesus is our rose. And we are his.

---

1. Antione De Saint Exupery, *The Little Prince* (USA: HJB Books, 1943; 1971), pp. 77-87.

2. "Lo, How A Rose E'er Blooming" translated by Theodore Baker, 1894. In the public domain.

Living By The Light We Have Known

O God, you have caused this night to shine with the brightness of the true Light: Grant that we, who have known the mystery of that light on earth, may also enjoy him perfectly in heaven....

— Collect for Christmas Eve

When our lives shine with the brightness of the true light, we know it. True light is unmistakable.

The scriptures tell us that all who were in the presence of the Christ Child were amazed — that's the word used to describe what it felt like to be there. They were amazed.

We know the feeling from the moments of sheer grace that come to us, when true light shines and we see, if only for a moment, as God sees. We are amazed. We know the feeling when our hearts are pierced and we love, if only for a moment, as God loves. Even more amazing, we feel ourselves loved as God loves us. We are amazed, in that moment, by the mysterious yet undeniable reality of God.

On this holy night, I invite you to consider what you know of the experience of Christ's coming, not in story long ago, but now, breaking through to us as light shining in darkness.

We know that Christ's coming will always be in and through ordinary things. "The miracle of God," writes the preacher, Peter Gomes, "is that he can make much out of nothing and something of almost anything."[1] Little things, as small as a gesture, a word, a gift of kindness, speak to us of grace and love. That's how Christ's coming works: not in big, flashy ways for all the world to see, but in the amazing moments when ordinary life shines with extraordinary brightness, when our hearts are warmed by gentle gifts of forgiveness and peace.

We also know that the true light of Christ's coming is, by design, a fleeting experience. It gives us a moment, not a lifetime, of clarity; a moment, not a lifetime, of joy or the capacity to bring joy to another. We are amazed and at once disappointed by this, because the light doesn't last long enough to really change things. Think of the shepherds returning to their flocks having heard the angels sing, while Mary and Joseph prepare to flee from the dangers of Herod. Surely we all wonder why the light doesn't stick around and overcome darkness once and for all.

Yet, the purpose of Christ's coming is never to change the world from the outside. Christ comes to change us from within so that we might live according to the glimpses of love we have known and that we might be channels of his light. Thus we needn't worry when the moment passes and we no longer feel as intently the power and presence of Christ's true light. That's how it is. The gift is no less real for its fleeting beauty.

I was at a nursing home recently visiting a dear friend who is slowly losing her cognitive abilities to Alzheimer's disease. In the forty minutes or so that we spoke, I understood almost nothing of what she said. I wasn't even sure if she knew who I was. Then as I began to take my leave, her eyes regained their familiar sparkle. She looked deeply into mine and told me that she loved me. She charged me to live my life in a very specific way that only she and I would understand, in light of past conversations. Then, just as quickly, her confusion and senseless ramblings returned. I left wondering what on earth had just happened. Did she actually say what I heard? It was amazing — a moment of true light and authentic love. Then it was gone, and I had a choice: Would I live as if that Christ moment between us had happened or not?

Which leads to yet another, more challenging truth we know of Christ's coming: it has to do with making room. The scriptures say that when Jesus was born there was no room for him. And for those with no room, there was no miracle. God invites us this night to make room. Make room for the miracles you have known. Claim them as the gifts that they are. Live by the glimpses of true light you have seen. Set your sights by that light, even when the darkness returns.

Whenever the true light of Christ comes to you in extraordinary ordinariness, be amazed. Make room. Hear the words spoken for you. Then go and live. Live from the truth, the love, and the light you have known.

----

1. Peter Gomes, "House of Bread," in *Sermons: Biblical Wisdom for Daily Living* (New York: William Morrow and Company, Inc., 1998), p. 23.

Epiphany 2, Year A or
Martin Luther King Jr. Sunday
Isaiah 49:1-7

What Shall Become Of The Dreamer's Dream?

And he said to me, "You are my servant, Israel, in whom I will be glorified." But I said, "I have labored in vain, I have spent my strength for nothing and vanity; yet surely my cause is with the Lord, and my reward with my God." And now the Lord says, who formed me in the womb to be his servant, to bring Jacob back to him, and that Israel might be gathered to him ... "It is too light a thing that you should be my servant to raise up the tribes of Jacob and to restore the survivors of Israel; I will give you as a light to the nations, that my salvation may reach to the end of the earth." Thus says the Lord ... to one deeply despised, abhorred by the nations, the slave of rulers, "Kings shall see and stand up, princes, and they shall prostrate themselves, because of the Lord, who is faithful, the Holy One of Israel, who has chosen you."   — Isaiah 49:3-7

The National Civil Rights Museum is built inside the old Lorraine Motel in Memphis, Tennessee, where Martin Luther King Jr. was assassinated on April 4, 1968. Hanging from the balcony where King died is an enormous fresh flower wreath and alongside it, a plaque inscribed with a passage from the biblical story in Genesis of Joseph's brothers plotting to get rid of him: "Here comes the dreamer. Come now, let us kill him ... and we shall see what will become of his dreams" (Genesis 37:19-20).

The museum is laid out as a walking tour, starting from the ground level, going in an upward spiral until you stand outside the room where King slept the last night of his life. The first floor is

93

dedicated to the historical antecedents of the Civil Rights Movement: slavery in the South, the Civil War, reconstruction, and white backlash against blacks throughout the latter nineteenth and early twentieth centuries. It highlights the importance of the black churches and of changes in mid-twentieth-century American society that laid the foundation of future struggles.

The first exhibit is devoted to the long legal effort to desegregate public schools, culminating in the historic 1954 Supreme Court decision, "Brown vs. the Board of Education in Topeka," that declared school segregation unconstitutional and subsequent showdowns between black students and the resisting white minority in places like Little Rock, Arkansas.

The next exhibit describes the movement to desegregate city buses in Montgomery, Alabama, which began when Rosa Parks refused to give up her seat when a white man demanded it. The exhibit has an actual bus you can get on, with a white section in the front, a Negro section in the back, and a statue of a black woman sitting down in the front. Rosa Parks is typically remembered as a woman too tired to stand up. She was, in fact, a quiet and determined young woman, the secretary of the local NAACP, strategically chosen to challenge bus segregation. The movement that followed was equally strategic in its planning.

Martin Luther King Jr., a newcomer in town, the 26-year-old pastor of Dexter Avenue Baptist Church, was elected leader of the Montgomery Improvement Association. He was more than ready for the challenge, having moved back to the South after his doctoral studies in Boston in order to be an agent of change. He devoted himself to the boycott, holding mass meetings, conducting training in nonviolence, and coordinating the million details associated with a protest that lasted over a year. What inspired him were the thousands of people who walked or carpooled everywhere they needed to go for 381 days. They walked and walked and walked. "My feet are tired," said one elderly woman on her way to clean houses on the white side of town, "but my soul is at rest."

The resistance, as you know, was fierce. King's home was bombed, and threats were made against his life and that of his wife and baby daughter. Others were harassed and beaten. Taxis were forbidden to pick up protesters and local companies cancelled the insurance of Negro car owners. King and his colleagues were arrested for violating hastily enacted anti-boycott laws. Indeed, King was due to be sentenced for his "crimes" on the day the US Supreme Court upheld a lower court's decision that Montgomery's bus segregation was unconstitutional.

Through it all, King kept an outward persona of calm and moral confidence, but the internal pressure was staggering. By the time the boycott was a month old, the Kings were receiving thirty to forty threatening phone calls and letters *each day*. One night, after he received a particularly vicious call, he paced the floors of his house wondering what to do. He went downstairs, made a cup of coffee, sat at the kitchen table, and prayed: "Lord, I am here taking a stand for what I believe is right. But Lord, I must confess that I'm weak now, I'm faltering. I'm losing my courage. Now, I am afraid. And I can't let the people see me like this. They are looking to me for leadership, and if I stand before them without strength and courage, they too will falter. I am at the end of my powers. I have nothing left. I've come to the point where I can't face it alone." In that lonely hour, King had the first transcendent experience of his life. He heard the quiet assurance of God's voice telling him to stand up for righteousness and truth. God would be at his side. With that, his uncertainty disappeared. He was ready to face anything.[1]

The next exhibit is dedicated to the student movement that organized sit-ins at lunch counters throughout the South. This was a spontaneous movement, born of the idealism and frustration of young people determined to change their lives. King, now the leader of the Southern Christian Leadership Conference and living in Atlanta, saw the power of their efforts and supported them however he could. He encouraged the young people to hold fast to nonviolence, no matter the violence that met them. In one year, the student movement successfully abolished lunch counter segregation in 27 cities.

The next exhibit highlights the Freedom Rides, again a student-led effort to desegregate interstate bus travel. This exhibit also has a bus, but you can't get on it. It's a burned-out shell, like several of the buses destroyed by angry mobs determined to do whatever was necessary to put black people in their place. Several people died in the Freedom Rides, hundreds were beaten and arrested. By 1961, the Interstate Commerce Commission posted signs on all buses and bus stations that banned segregation.

A large exhibit is dedicated to the 1963 campaign to challenge a full range of segregation laws in Birmingham, Alabama, a place with more unsolved bombings of black homes and churches than anywhere in the country and where police brutality reigned. The Birmingham campaign, like the one in Montgomery, was carefully organized, beginning small and working up to larger and larger nonviolent protests. King was again jailed. This was where he wrote his now famous "Letter from a Birmingham Jail" in response to local religious leaders who openly criticized his work. King expressed his disappointment in them, white church leaders throughout the South. "I once hoped," he wrote, "that white ministers, priests, and rabbis of the South would be among our strongest allies. Instead, some have been outright opponents. All too many others have been more cautious than courageous and have remained silent behind the anesthetizing security of stained-glass windows."[2]

Courage came, yet again, from the ranks of children and young people. When the protests began to falter in Birmingham, King encouraged the leadership to go the schools and universities and invited the youth to march. March they did, in numbers defying expectation, against the caution of their parents and teachers. It would be called the "Children's Miracle" as some as young as eight walked, allowing themselves to be beaten by policemen and their dogs. "Don't worry about your children," King told a group of concerned parents. "Don't hold them back if they want to go to jail. For they are doing a job not only for themselves but for all America and all mankind. They are carving a tunnel of hope through the great mountain of despair...."[3]

I bought a poster from the Civil Rights Museum titled, "Courage," with a black and white photograph of three young people being pushed into a brick wall by a fire hose. Below the photo is the definition: "Courage — the mental and moral strength to venture, persevere, and withstand fear and difficulty."

The years 1963-1965 represent the high point of the Civil Rights Movement in terms of momentum and accomplishment. In August 1963, King stood on the steps of the Lincoln Memorial to share the power of his dream. In 1964, the Civil Rights Act was passed, the Mississippi Freedom Summer brought civil rights activists from around the country to help register black people to vote, and King was awarded the Nobel Peace Prize. In 1965, there was an extraordinary 4,000-person march from Selma to Montgomery, a distance of 54 miles, to protest voting rights violations in Selma, and President Johnson signed the Voting Rights Act into law. Yet, for every moment of glory, came another round of violence. Just two weeks after the march on Washington, four little girls died in a church bombing in Birmingham, and King preached at their funeral. Others, too, were murdered. King's life was threatened so many times that he lost count. Hundreds were arrested in Selma and subjected to intense brutality. Several civil rights leaders were killed, including James Reeb, a white minister and Viola Liuzzo, a white mother from Detroit, who was overtaken by the Ku Klux Klan as she was driving in her car.

King wrote of the march from Selma to Montgomery as the highlight of his life. Thousands of people from around the nation had come to participate. King had issued a call to the religious leaders of America, and this time the churches responded, gloriously, courageously, as hundreds of ministers, priests, and rabbis climbed into their pulpits, declared that they themselves were going south and invited others to join them. The people that you and I know who said, "Yes," some of whom are sitting in these pews, still speak of those events as among the most significant of their lives. The Dutch priest, Henri Nouwen, was a graduate student in Topeka, Kansas, at the time. He climbed into his Volkswagen and headed south. He stopped outside Vicksburg, Tennessee, to pick up a black hitchhiker, a twenty-year-old man named Charles. Charles exclaimed, "God has heard my prayer. He sent you as an angel from heaven. I've been standing here for hours and no one would pick me up. The white men have all tried to run me off the road. But I made a cross in the road and prayed to God that he would allow me to go to Selma to help my people. He heard my prayer."[4]

King's life was threatened as he prepared to lead the march. The Justice Department warned King that a sniper was planning to shoot him and that King should drop out of the march. King said that he would march out in front. Andrew Young came up with a creative solution. Figuring that all black people look the same to whites, he invited all the black ministers wearing dark suits to join King in front. About forty did, and they led the march into Montgomery without incident.[5]

The museum's last exhibits are filled with the confusion and controversies of King's last years, as the tide of public opinion, both white and black, began to turn against him. The decisions he made in those years remain the subject of much debate. His decision to move to Chicago and highlight the perniciousness of racism in the North and his decision to focus on issues of poverty and the economic discrimination against all poor people are still debated. His decision to speak out, at long last, against the Vietnam War and in so doing incur the wrath of his once great ally, President Johnson and the decision to go to Memphis to support the Negro sanitation workers in their poorly organized and doomed-to-fail strike for decent working conditions are still debated.

Many whites felt he had overstepped his bounds. Many blacks believed his nonviolent views were woefully inadequate in the face of escalating violence against them. But King pressed on. He said, "The ultimate measure of a man is not where he stands in moments of convenience, but where he stands in moments of challenge, crisis and controversy. The cross is something you bear and ultimately you die on."

The night before King died, he spoke at a church in Memphis. His close friend and colleague, Andrew Young, said that the reality of his death was all around him that night. Young said that when he spoke, King preached the fear of death right out of him.

The last part of his sermon is well known. In it he tells the congregation that God has allowed him to go the mountaintop, look over, and see the promised land. "I may not get there with you," he said, "but I am here to tell that we, as a people, will get to the promised land."

The first part of the sermon is equally compelling. He begins with a statement of heart-breaking candor: "I guess one of the great agonies of life is that we are constantly trying to finish that which is unfinishable. We are commanded to do that. And so we find ourselves in so many instances having to face the fact that our dreams are not fulfilled. Life is a continual story of shattered dreams.

> *Each one of you in some way is building some kind of temple. The struggle is always there. It gets discouraging sometimes. Some of us are trying to build a temple of peace. We speak out against war, we protest, but it seems to mean nothing. And so often as you set out to build the temple of peace you are left lonesome, discouraged and bewildered. Well, that is the story of life. And the thing that makes me happy is that I can hear a voice crying through the vista of time, saying, "It may not come today or it may not come tomorrow but it's good that it is within your heart. It's good that you are trying. You may not see it. The dream may not be fulfilled, but it's just good that you have a desire to bring it into reality."*[6]

He also gave an interpretation of the parable of the Good Samaritan that epitomizes how King lived his life, from those early days in Montgomery right to the end. He began by contrasting the actions of the priest and the Levite who passed the wounded man on the roadside with that of the Samaritan who stopped and offered help.

> *I think those men were afraid. And so the first question the priest and Levite asked was, "If I stop to help this man, what will happen to me?" But the Good Samaritan reversed the question: "If I do not stop to help this man, what will happen to him?" That's the question before you tonight. Not, "If I stop to help the sanitation workers, what will happen to my job, or my normal duties as a pastor?" The question is not, "If I stop to help people in need, what will happen to me?" The*

*question is "If I do not stop to help the sanitation work-
ers, what will happen to them?" That's the question.*[7]

For those of us called to follow Jesus, in our moment of this
country's history, it's our question, too.
King was shot as he left his hotel room and headed down the
balcony stairs to go to dinner. His last question to Andrew Young
was if the singer, Mahalia Jackson, was going to be there, and if so,
if he would ask her to sing his favorite hymn: "Precious Lord."
Mahalia Jackson didn't sing anything that night, but she sang it for
King's funeral five days later.

---

1. Clayborne Carson, editor, *The Autobiography of Martin Luther King, Jr.* (New York: Warner Books, 1998), p. 77.

2. Martin Luther King Jr., "Letter from a Birmingham Jail," from *A Testament Of Hope: The Essential Writings and Speeches of Martin Luther King Jr.*, James M. Washington, editor (New York: HarperOne, 1990), p. 199.

3. *Op cit*, Carson, "Statement at a Birmingham Mass Meeting," p. 211.

4. Richard Deats, *Martin Luther King: Spirit-Led Prophet* (New York: New City Press, 2003), p. 101.

5. *Ibid*, p. 103.

6. *Op cit*, Martin Luther King Jr., "I See The Promised Land," p. 284.

7. *Ibid*, p. 285.

Epiphany 6, Year B
2 Kings 5:1-14
Mark 1:40-45

Where Healing And Acceptance Meet

Naaman, commander of the army of the king of Aram, was a great man and in high favor with his master, because by him the Lord had given victory to Aram. The man, though a mighty warrior, suffered from leprosy. Now the Arameans on one of their raids had taken a young girl captive from the land of Israel, and she served Naaman's wife. She said to her mistress, "If only my lord were with the prophet who is in Samaria! He would cure him of his leprosy." So Naaman went in and told his lord just what the girl from the land of Israel had said. And the king of Aram said, "Go then, and I'll send along a letter to the King of Israel." He went, taking with him ten talents of silver, six thousand shekels of gold, and ten sets of garments.... So Naaman came with his horses and chariots, and halted at the entrance of Elisha's house. Elisha sent a messenger to him, saying, "Go, wash in the Jordan seven times, and your flesh shall be restored and you shall be clean." But Naaman became angry and went away, saying, "I thought that for me he would surely come out, and stand and call on the name of Lord his God, and would wave his hand over the spot, and cure the leprosy! Are not Abana and Pharpar, the rivers of Damascus, better than all the waters of Israel? Could I not wash in them, and be clean?" He turned and went away in a rage. But his servants approached and said to him, "Father, if the prophet had commanded you to do something difficult, would you not have done it? How much more, when all he said was, 'Wash, and be clean'?" So he went down

101

and immersed himself seven times in the Jordan, according to the word of the man of God; his flesh was restored like the flesh of a young boy, and he was clean.
— 2 Kings 5:1-5, 9-14

A leper came to him begging him, and kneeling he said to him, "If you choose, you can make me clean." Moved with pity, Jesus stretched out his hand and touched him, and said to him, "I do choose. Be made clean!" Immediately the leprosy left him, and he was made clean. After sternly warning him he sent him away at once, saying to him, "See that you say nothing to anyone; but go, show yourself to the priest, and offer for your cleansing what Moses commanded, as a testimony to them." But he went out and began to proclaim it freely, and to spread the word, so that Jesus could no longer go into a town openly, but stayed out in the country; and people came to him from every quarter.
— Mark 1:40-45

Healing begins with acceptance. We can't change anything about ourselves or our surroundings unless we first accept it. To walk the path of healing, we must first make our peace with whatever it is — in, among, or around us — that needs to be healed.

Acceptance, as you know, is not easy. Those in recovery can attest to the years of denial that typically precede making that first step: admitting that we are powerless over whatever it is that has us in its grip. Similarly, when confronted with a difficult diagnosis or other evidence that something about us is not well, we can't take it in at first. Our minds will do almost anything to keep difficult truth at bay.

As the truth penetrates our well-fortified consciousness, we then easily fall into familiar ruts of shame, guilt, or blame. When my mother was diagnosed with cancer in her jaw last year, her instinctual reaction was to blame herself, to wonder what she had done in her life to cause this disease. Did she not brush her teeth properly? Was it those cigarettes she smoked, briefly, as a young adult trying to look sophisticated? Was she being punished for something she had said or done? Her thinking was completely irrational, but I recognized it. "What did I do wrong?" is a natural response to suffering, as is, on the opposite extreme, asking, "What did someone else do to make me this way?" In other words, "Whose fault is this?"

Healing begins with acceptance — not just acceptance of the disease, addiction, or whatever it is that we wish were not true about us but of our very selves. To heal we must accept ourselves, as we are, broken in all the places that we are broken; impaired in all the ways we are impaired. Acceptance takes us to that deep place where we know ourselves to be flawed in particular, undeniable ways and, in our impairment, unconditionally loved by God. From that place, and that place alone, can we begin to love ourselves for who we are and others as they are, wounds, warts, and all.

Jesus' tremendous healing power flowed from his unconditional acceptance of every person he met as a beloved child of God. He never defined people according to their sin or sickness, but saw them in their entirety, as God saw them. He rejected the rigid purity codes that judged sick people as spiritually unclean. Those with leprosy were particularly isolated in his day, forced to live on the borders of human society, required to cry out their condition whenever another person approached, and obliged to endure condemnation for their supposed depravity. Jesus would have none of that. When lepers approached him, as did the man in today's story, he engaged them as precious human beings. He looked into their eyes and saw them; he reached out to touch them. He was, as the scriptures say, moved to compassion by their plight, and he treated them with dignity. That is to say, he accepted and loved them. And from that acceptance and love, they were healed.

Sometimes the only healing we get is acceptance, which is hard to imagine settling for when what we really want is to be released from whatever afflicts us. A dear friend who has made peace with her paralysis and lives a rich, full life from the confinement of a wheelchair told me that those who are just facing a similar fate don't want to hear how she had found that peace. "They don't want to accept what I have accepted. They want to walk

103

again," she said, "and I don't blame them." Sometimes the healing we are given is acceptance of our lot, whatever that is, and when acceptance takes us to that deep spiritual place where we are known and loved by God, acceptance is enough. There's a story told about an old rabbi who lost his sight and could no longer read or see the faces of those who came to visit him. A faith healer approached him and said, "Entrust your life into my care and I will heal your blindness." "That won't be necessary," the rabbi replied, "I can see all that I need to."

Buddhism has much to teach about the spirituality of acceptance. A sacred Buddhist principle is the acceptance of suffering, discomfort, and tension as part of life. "There is no cure for hot and cold," Buddhists will say. There is no way around the difficulties and heartaches that make us human. Suffering is not the result of a mistake you made; it's not a punishment. To accept suffering is the first step toward freedom.

The American Buddhist nun, Pema Chodron, in a book aptly titled *The Wisdom of No Escape*, wrote this:

> *The mistake that keeps us caught in our own particular kind of ignorance, unkindness and shut-downness is that we are never encouraged to see clearly what is, with gentleness. Instead, we imagine that we should try to be better than we already are, that we should try to improve ourselves, that we should try to get away from painful things, and that if we could just get away from the painful things, then we would be happy.*
>
> *Meditation is about seeing clearly the body that we have, the mind that we have, the domestic situation that we have, the job that we have, and the people who are in our lives ... It's not about trying to become better than we are, but just seeing clearly with precision and gentleness ... The only way to do this is to be open, and develop some sense of sympathy for everything that comes along, and let it teach you what it will.*[1]

When we can accept and learn from what causes us pain, then in a profound way we are healed from it, even if the pain persists.

Saint Paul came to that kind of acceptance in his life when he asked to be healed from a particularly distracting and disabling condition. We don't know what the condition was, only that he called it "... a thorn given to him in the flesh, to keep him from being too elated. Three times I appealed to the Lord about this, that it would leave me, but the Lord said to me, 'My grace is sufficient for you, for power is made perfect in weakness ...' " (2 Corinthians 12:7-9).

Yet there is another truth, one that seems to contradict all that I've said thus far. That truth, revealed to us in the healing stories of the Bible and of our own lives, is that sometimes — perhaps even most times — healing begins in acceptance and continues on to full recovery, renewal of life, and transformation of relationships. We needn't simply accept our wounds; sometimes, by the grace and mercy of God, we are fully healed of them, our souls and bodies stronger, as they say, in the broken places. Sometimes the blind receive their sight. Sometimes the lame walk; the sorrowful rejoice; the oppressed go free.

I don't pretend to understand the mystery of healing. I only know that it's true. I hold out for the possibility in every area of my life where I struggle to accept the pain and brokenness that is mine, and even where I have succeeded in that acceptance. I pray the same for others — for you, those we love, and for our troubled and beautiful world.

The biblical story of Naaman, the mighty Aramean warrior afflicted with leprosy, is a brilliant treatise on healing. Naaman is one of my favorite biblical characters: a strong warrior afflicted with a dreaded disease. He wanted to be well. When he heard of the possibility of healing from a foreign prophet, he set out at once, bringing all the gold and silver he could carry, to appease both the king and the prophet of Israel. But when Elisha told him what the Lord required for his healing — washing seven times in the Jordan River — Naaman was incensed. He wanted more than that! He wanted his healing to be dramatic, worthy of the effort he had made. And were it not for the courage of his servant, challenging him with one of the best questions in the Bible, he might have missed the healing available to him: "If the prophet had commanded you to do something difficult, would you not have done it? How much more, when all he said was, 'Wash and be clean?' "

What might our equivalent of Naaman's resistance be, the thing we are slow to accept or believe in because it doesn't seem like enough?

For me the answer is time. Healing takes time. And I don't want to hear that when faced with an urgent condition of suffering or sorrow, ruptured relationship or grief. I want healing now. But what if time is essential to healing? What if we can't rush the process along, anymore than we can make a bean grow faster, as my teacher used to say, by pulling on it?

A few years ago, I experienced my first, rather severe, case of tendonitis at the place where my foot meets my shin. I didn't recognize the pain and for a long time I ignored it, thinking I had stretched a muscle. As it worsened, I continued my normal routines of movement and exercise until I couldn't walk. When I finally sought help, the doctor told me that there was nothing I could do but rest my foot. The more I walked on it, he said, the longer it would take to heal. "How long would it take?" I asked.

He replied, "About two months."

It was the longest two months of my life. I would have done anything to heal faster. But what my body needed was time — time and rest. Whenever I tried to rush the process along, I only set myself back.

Wounds take time to heal. Rabbi Edwin Friedman writes of a woman dealing with various problems of loss — divorce from her husband, separating from her children, and changes in her relationship with her mother. She was a nurse and she came across a description in a medical journal about physical healing that helped her with her emotional struggles:

> When a wound occurs, there are two kinds of tissue that must heal, the connective tissue below the surface, and the protective tissue of the skin. If the protective tissue heals too quickly, healing of the connective tissue will not be sound, causing other problems to surface later, or worse, never to surface at all.[2]

She was able to make the analogy to the wounds in her family, realizing the danger in allowing the surface to heal too quickly, foregoing the possibility of deeper healing later on.

So often when a wound occurs our inclination is to rush in and try to fix it. But perhaps what's needed is to put our helpful impulses aside and allow time to do its work. "Time and showing up," writes Anne Lamott, "turns most messes into compost." In an essay about learning to raise an adolescent son, Lamott acknowledges that sometimes the two of them are simply a mess. "But that is usually where any hope of improvement begins, acknowledging the mess. When I am well, I know not to mess with mess right away; I try to let silence and time work their magic."[3]

That, I suggest to you, is where acceptance and healing meet: in that place where we open ourselves to the healing grace of God, wanting to be well, reconciled, and transformed, while at the same time recognizing that all healing takes time. In the meantime, in that in-between place where we live most of our lives, we'll be all right. We can learn to live with imperfections. We can mine them for all they have to teach. In so doing, we'll discover the greatest healing truth of all: that we are beloved of God, right now, as we are. In time, all will be well. But in the meantime, God's grace is sufficient for us, and we can live with peace and joy, love and purpose, as we are, right now.

---

1. Pema Chodron, *The Wisdom of No Escape* (Boston: Shambhala Press, 2001), pp. 14, 32.

2. Edwin Friedman, *Generation to Generation: Family Process in Church and Synagogue* (New York: The Guilford Press, 1985), pp. 42-44.

3. Anne Lamott, "Holy of Holies," and "Adolescence," in *Plan B: Further Thoughts on Faith* (New York: Riverhead Books, 2005), pp. 76, 100.

Ash Wednesday
Isaiah 58:1-12
2 Corinthians 5:20b—6:10
Matthew 6:1-6, 16-21

Forty Days — A Long Time But Not Too Long

The Lord will guide you continually, and satisfy your needs in parched places, and make your bones strong; and you shall be like a watered garden, like a spring of water, whose waters never fail. Your ancient ruins shall be rebuilt; you shall raise up the foundations of many generations; you shall be called the repairer of the breach, the restorer of streets to live in.
— Isaiah 58:11-12

See, now is the acceptable time; see, now is the day of salvation! — 2 Corinthians 6:2c

For where your treasure is, there your heart will be also. — Matthew 6:21

The season of Lent is a fixed period of time — forty days — counting backward from Easter Sunday (skipping Sundays) to mark its beginning, always on a Wednesday, which we call Ash in reference to the ashes we will shortly place on our foreheads as a reminder of our mortality. The reason Lent moves around in the calendar year, some years coming as early as the first week in February, other years not beginning until mid-March, is that Easter, unlike Christmas, is not a fixed date. It moves around according to the rhythms of the sun and the moon. Easter Day falls on the first Sunday after the full moon that occurs on or after the spring equinox.

The forty days of Lent are patterned after the great biblical rhythms of forty — the forty years the people of Israel wandered

109

in the wilderness before entering the promised land; the forty days Jesus spent in his own wilderness, in prayer, fasting, and spiritual preparation before beginning his public ministry. Forty is a symbolic number in the Bible. It signifies a long time. Forty days is long enough that if we are to do anything consistently in that time, we will have to think about it. It will take effort and intention. If we rely on our feelings alone — whether or not we *feel* like doing something, chances are good we won't make it for forty days. Yet, forty days is not forever. Lent is a long enough period of time to get our attention but not so long that we can't see past it.

Given that Lent is essentially time, I ask you to consider with me our experience of time. "What is time?" Saint Augustine asked sixteen centuries ago. "Provided no one asks me, I know. If I want to explain it to an inquirer, I do not know."[1]

In her book, *Receiving the Day*, Christian author, Dorothy C. Bass, wrote:

> *Time is a given and time is a gift. We receive it in increments that flow from the past into the future, a certain number of hours each day, a certain number of days each year, a certain span of life whose duration we do not know in advance. Making good use of the time we are given is important, to be sure, and date books and other aids can help us do this. But when our emphasis on using time displaces our awareness of time as a gift, we find that we are not so much using time as permitting time to use us. That is what is happening to more and more of us, more and more often.*[2]

How might we think about time this Lent, and reclaim the gift of it, whether the hours stretch out slowly, marked by boredom or pain, or whether the days fly by, unnoticed in the frenzy of all that we feel we must accomplish?

We have friends who teach in a boarding school, which is as complex and busy a work setting as I have ever witnessed. Their schedules whirl around nearly constant obligations, not merely of teaching, but of surrogate parenting, dorm duty, coaching, grading papers, and administration. The great compensation for them is, of course, the long stretch of summer vacation. "But what kind of life is it," one of them once asked me, "if I am simply enduring whole chunks of time throughout the year just to arrive at summer? I feel as if I am willing away my life." Clearly, she needed to find a way to cherish the gift of all her time, not merely the three months she didn't teach. How can we do something of the same, receive each day as a gift, and not rush through or feel we must simply endure precious portions of the only life we have?

Here is where spiritual practice can help us, by giving us the means to mark the days — starting with these forty days of Lent. Spiritual practice needn't be a complex, time-consuming endeavor. It can be as simple as waking up and at some moment in those early hours pausing to give thanks. "This is the day the Lord has made," writes the psalmist, "let us be glad and rejoice in it." And at day's end, we might pause again, looking back on our experience. "How was your day?" we often ask one another in greeting. What if we plumbed that question a bit? How *was* your day? What good or hard things happened? What are you grateful for? What are you struggling with or what do you regret? Where did you meet God or feel touched by grace?

Another simple spiritual practice is to consider a question or struggle or dream that lives on the edges of our consciousness, the things we think about as we're drifting off to sleep, or worry about beneath the surface, or hope for, perhaps in secret. Whatever it is, we can simply devote a few minutes each day and bring it to the surface, considering the question, the struggle, or the dream, opening ourselves to God, and allowing ourselves, bit by bit, to live into its truth. This is what someone once called "back burner thinking," slow and steady, in the midst of doing other things.

I was making a pot of soup while writing these thoughts. I put the pot on early and added ingredients over time. For several hours all I did was get up periodically and stir the pot. While I was doing other things, the soup was still cooking. I wonder if the "slow cooking" of the important questions, struggles, or dreams we carry isn't like that, too. Eventually we will find clarity, or be shown a path,

111

or experience forgiveness, but in the meantime, all we may need to do is stir the pot and let God work while we're doing other things. My spiritual practice this Lent will be reclaiming the gift of time. I intend to begin each morning with a brief prayer of thanks, inspired by the practice of many African-American Christians to pray words like, "Thank you, God, for waking me up this morning, for putting shoes on my feet, clothes on my back, and food on my table. Thank you, God, for health and strength and the activities of my limbs. Thank you that I awoke in my right mind, mostly."[3]

Then in the evening, or at the end of the day, I intend to look back and reflect on where I found joy, where I struggled or experienced pain, where I met God, or was touched by grace. And, I intend to keep track of the questions of my heart, each day, in writing.

Let me end with a poem by the Sufi mystic, Rumi, which speaks powerfully of God's sense of time with and for us:

> *I have come to drag you out of yourself and take you to*
> *my heart.*
> *I have come to bring out the beauty you never knew*
> *you had, and lift you like a prayer to the sky.*
> *If no one else recognizes you, I do, because you are my*
> *heart and my soul.*
> *Don't run away, accept your wounds, and let bravery*
> *be your shield.*
> *It takes a thousand years for the perfect being to evolve.*
> *Every step of the way I will walk with you and never*
> *leave you stranded.*
> *Be patient; do not open the lid too soon.*
> *Simmer away, until you are ready.*[4]

---

1. Quoted in *Receiving the Day: Christian Practices for Opening the Gift of Time,* by Dorothy C. Bass (San Francisco: Jossey-Bass Publishers, 2000), p. viii.

2. *Ibid*, p. 2.

3. *Ibid*, p. 19.

4. Maryam Mafi, *Rumi: Hidden Music* (London: Thorsons, 2002), p. 147.

You, Too, Can Be Born Again

> *There was a Pharisee named Nicodemus, a leader of the Jews. He came to Jesus by night and said to him, "Rabbi, we know that you are a teacher who has come from God; for no one can do these signs that you do apart from the presence of God." Jesus answered him, "Very truly, I tell you, no one can see the kingdom of God without being born from above."* — John 3:1-3

Neal Karlen is a nationally known journalist based in Minneapolis. He grew up a devout and passionate Jew, but for a variety of reasons, along the path of young adulthood, he lost his faith — completely — and he lost himself, too.

At age forty he "hit bottom," as it were, and the reality of his life hit him like a ton of bricks. He didn't like who he had become, a parody of a Jew among his Gentile friends. To borrow from Dante's *Inferno*, Karlen found himself midway on life's journey, in a dark wood, the right road lost. During that difficult time he met, on an airplane of all places, a Hasidic rabbi from the Lubavitcher sect — someone, from a Jewish perspective, on the extreme fringes of faith. As they talked, Karlen sensed with the instincts of a desperate man that this was someone who could help him. Like Nicodemus coming to Jesus by night, Karlen decided in his darkest hour to ask if the rabbi would help him. The rabbi agreed.

Thus began their unlikely friendship. The rabbi listened intently to Karlen's long list of woes. The first thing he did was suggest that Karlen lighten up a bit and stop taking himself so seriously. "People often come to me," he said, "at the point of suicide. They tell me, 'My life has no meaning, my family counts for nothing; I'm a terrible human being,' the usual. And I say, 'Why stop there? Why not stick around and at least come up with a full list?

You're also boring, unpleasant, a terrible friend, and your jokes aren't funny.' "

"That gets them laughing, too," he said, "which usually gives them the distance to see that the world does not revolve around them. Yet at the same time I want to impress upon them that God needs them. Even in their present state, when they feel so broken and insignificant, God needs their good deeds, done their particular way, with all their faults and shortcomings."

That was the end of their first meeting. The rabbi sent Karlen home with two instructions: to read the Torah portion allotted for each week, and to bring in his *tefillin*, the armband that signals one is a Jew. No matter that Karlen no longer believed in God. It was as if the rabbi knew that salvation lay not in proper belief or how we feel or what we think we know about God, but rather in life practice, what the Archbishop of Canterbury calls "the shape of our lives and the habits of our hearts."

So it went: They would meet weekly, study the Torah together, and talk. Karlen occasionally joined the rabbi's family for meals, allowing the warmth of their affection to wash over him. Slowly, through the daily practice of his tradition and this friendship with an eccentric rabbi, Karlen's life, and eventually his faith, came back to him, or rather, emerged in a new way. He was born again, out of the ashes of a life that had died. It didn't happen all at once. There were no flashes of brilliance and no shortcuts. One day the rabbi encouraged him to do the very thing he had been dreading most: obey the Fourth Commandment. "Go home," the rabbi told him. "Find a way to honor your father." And Karlen did.

After they had been meeting for about a year, the rabbi spoke to Karlen about the ancient, mystical path of the Kabbalah. The Kabbalah describes the emotions of life and disciplines of the heart that lead us from ourselves, to the love of others, and at last to the healing of the world out of love for God. Hear what he had to say, in light of Jesus' words to Nicodemus about the need to be born from above, or born again, born of the Spirit.

We begin all aspects of life, the rabbi said, with animated emotions such as *love*, *fear*, and *compassion*. These are the emotions that move us, filling our lives with drama. Every good book is about them. Every human relationship starts off with them, as does our relationship with God. They are the emotions of energy and passion.

Yet if we are to mature in life and in love, we must go deeper, to other emotions not nearly as exciting as the first. They are, however, what determines how well we will love when the passion is gone. They are *perseverance*, *discipline*, and *humility*. With them we are able to shift our focus away from ourselves — how we feel and what we want — to concern for others and what is best for them.

Finally, he said, there are the deepest emotions of all that unite us to God. The first of these is *gratitude*, which enables us to acknowledge, in the midst of everything that happens, that our lives are a gift from God. I think of the words of one of our Eucharistic prayers: "It is right and good and a joyful thing at all times and in all places to give thanks to you, Creator of heaven and earth." Finally, there is *self-sacrifice*, the willingness to die so that others might live, the ways parents die a little each day to give life to their children, the way so many give sacrificially for others' sake, the way we Christians understand what Jesus has done for us.[1]

I tell you of Neal Karlen and his wonderful rabbi because I believe so strongly in what the rabbi taught him. I believe that when Jesus spoke of our need to be born anew and born of the Spirit, he was talking about the kind of painstaking spiritual transformation that Karlen experienced, gradually, over time. It is one of the most powerful metaphors of our faith — that the spiritual life is a kind of birth, a birth that follows death, dying to one way of being and rising to another.

I think it's safe to say that Christians divide themselves into two camps according to their comfort level with this notion of being born again. For some, it is the best way to describe what happened to them when they surrendered to God and invited Jesus into their heart, or to account for some other dramatic experience that changed them, personally and spiritually. For others, however, the concept of being born again is too narrow, too focused on one particular religious experience, and wrapped up in a worldview that they simply can't accept. Or, as Marcus Borg pointed out in his book, *The Heart of Christianity*, many are turned away by the example of others who are born again in a "particularly unattractive way." But he is clear about the distortion: "When being born again leads to a rigid kind of righteousness, judgmentalism, and sharp boundaries between an in-group and an out-group, it's either not a genuine born again experience or it has a lot of static in it."[2]

We do ourselves a great disservice if we allow such distortions to prevent us from living into the power of this profound religious experience. For to be born anew, born of Spirit, is to be touched by the power of the living God and moved by God to a transformation of life. For some, the born again experience is dramatic. For others, being born again is a gradual, incremental process, such as Karlen's slow and steady transformation under the influence of a spiritually wise rabbi. It simply takes time.

Even if we have profound emotional experiences as part of our life in God — and I pray that we all do — in the end, they will not sustain us. They are like falling in love, they are rooted in passion. We can go a long way on passion, of course, and who wouldn't want to? But for spiritual transformation to take root in us, we need to bring certain intentionality to our faith. Faith — our life in God — is not a feeling, or an affirmation of certain belief statements. Faith is about how we live when the feelings are gone; how we love when we don't feel loving, how we cultivate, even when we don't feel like it, the practice of gratitude and self-giving. Being born again requires that we die to something, that we let go of whatever it is holding us back on the path to becoming more like God.

Make no mistake: This kind of life transformation isn't something we do. It is the work of the Holy Spirit. Whether it happens suddenly or gradually, we can't make it happen by willing it, wanting it, or parroting what we think are the right things to say. We can be intentional about our relationship with God. The relationship already exists: God lives within us whether or not we realize or acknowledge it. Spiritual practice is waking up, paying attention, and allowing God more room to work through us.

In Zen Buddhism the story is told of a young professor who visits a Zen master asking to receive enlightenment. The master offers the young professor a cup of tea. He pours the tea into an empty cup. He continues pouring even after the teacup is full and the tea spills over the edge and fills the saucer. The master continues pouring. As the tea spills onto the floor, the young professor is no longer able to contain himself. "Stop!" he cries, "it can't hold anymore." "Exactly like you," the master replies. "How can you be open to receive enlightenment when you are already so full of yourself?"[3]

Being born again is something like having our cup emptied so that God can fill it. It can happen all at once when life turns on a dime, or when a series of choices or events lead us to an acute awareness of our need. Think of Karlen's moment of desperation when he first reached out to the rabbi. At other times, emptying our cup is more like what Martin Luther wrote of centuries ago — a *daily* dying to self so that Christ might enter in. This is the process of transformation the rabbi spoke of from the Kabbalah — making room by paying attention to the things we would rather avoid, acknowledging the ways we react defensively when others speak the truth, blaming others for our own unhappiness, flaring up in anger when we don't get what we want, panicking when we feel we're losing control, focusing on the sins of others rather than looking into our own hearts, or filling our days with so many distractions that we don't have to think or pray or spend time with those we love. This is daily emptying, making room, so that God can change us. It isn't easy.

Remember what the good rabbi said: First of all, lighten up. As important as we are, the universe does not revolve around us. Second, the practice of faith is more important than our feelings about faith. The habits of our hearts are what sustain us. The spiritual life isn't meant to be lived alone. Find yourself a teacher, a spiritual guide, or find a group of people with whom you can explore the questions of your heart.

Remember what Jesus said: God does not condemn us. God longs to show us a way and to be our companion in all that happens. But God is also about the work of our transformation, freeing us to love, to give, and to serve, in our own imperfect and glorious ways. That work has already begun in you and in me. The hardest part is emptying our cup and letting go of whatever needs to die. Do you know what it is? Do you know what you're hanging onto that God is asking you to surrender? To let go feels like dying, I know. On the other side of that death is life. There is abundant life for us on the other side.

---

1. Neal Karlen, *Shanda: The Making and Breaking of a Self-Loathing Jew* (New York: Simon & Schuster, 2004).

2. Marcus Borg, *The Heart of Christianity: Discovering a Life of Faith* (San Francisco: HarperSanFrancisco, 2003), p. 104.

3. Quoted by Thomas R. Hawkins in *The Learning Congregation* (Louisville: Westminster Knox Press, 1997), p. 33.

The Antidote To Anger

The Passover of the Jews was near, and Jesus went up to Jerusalem. In the temple he found people selling cattle, sheep, and doves, and the money changers seated at their tables. Making a whip of cords, he drove all of them out of the temple, both the sheep and the cattle. He also poured out the coins of the money changers and overturned their tables. He told those who were selling the doves, "Take these things out of here! Stop making my Father's house a market place!" His disciples remembered that it was written, "Zeal for your house will consume me." The Jews then said to him, "What sign can you show us for doing this?" Jesus answered them, "Destroy the temple, and in three days I will raise it up." The Jews then said, "This temple has been under construction for forty-six years, and will you raise it in three days?" But he was speaking of the temple of his body. After he was raised from the dead, his disciples remembered that he had said this; and they believed the scripture and the word that Jesus had spoken. — John 2:13-22*

The Academy Award winning film for Best Picture of 2005, *Crash*, tells the complicated story of race relations in America, with a car crash on the streets of Los Angeles as its central metaphor. *Crash* is also a story about anger. Nearly every character in the film is angry — legitimately angry — about something. The tragedy lies in the way their anger spills over from one realm of life to another, setting off ripple effects of violence that spread far beyond their awareness or intention.

There is a brilliant young African-American man who is angry at all things associated with white privilege. In response, he chooses a life of crime that he convinces himself is principled, even ethical, because he only steals from white people.

There is a Persian shop owner who believes that everyone in this country is out to cheat him, and he is angry at those who break into his shop and steal. We watch him attempting to buy a gun in a weapons shop run by a white man who is still angry about what happened to our country on September 11. The shop owner sees in the Persian man all those responsible for those heinous crimes. You can imagine what their conversation was like.

There is a white police officer who harbors deep resentment for the way his father was economically destroyed by city policies favoring minority-owned businesses. He's also angry at the way his father is now subjected to substandard medical care administered by an inept health maintenance organization that won't allow his father to be treated for what is probably prostate cancer. The policeman takes out his anger on a wealthy African-American couple he stops on the highway, in a clear case of racially motivated police harassment and, with the woman, sexual abuse.

There is the genteel African-American television director whom the white policeman pulls over. He seems to live a gracious and enlightened life until you realize how he has paid for that life with a steady diet of humiliation. He isn't quick to anger, but the poisonous way he is treated eats at his soul until he finally reaches a breaking point of rage.

There is the upper middle-class woman kept in an affluent lifestyle by her husband, the District Attorney for the City of Los Angeles, who is probably sleeping with his assistant, is never home, and who treats his wife alternately as a trophy and a child.

In one scene this woman is speaking to a friend on the telephone a few days after she and her husband were attacked and had their car stolen. She says to her friend, "I am so angry. I'm angry at my husband, at the housekeeper, at the man at the dry cleaners who ruined yet another silk blouse, and at the gardener for overwatering the lawn. I keep on thinking that one day I'm going to wake up feeling better. But then I realized that how I feel has nothing to do with our car being stolen. I wake up like this every day. I am angry all the time and I don't know why."

What do you do with your anger? How do you know when you're angry and how do you communicate your anger to others? Are you one with a long, slow fuse, able to take a lot before things get to you, or are you more volatile? Do you respond to what angers you with anger, or with another, more acceptable emotion? Does expressing anger truly release it, or does expression simply serve to rehearse anger, hone it to perfection, as it takes up more room both within and around us? Does anger serve a purpose, and if so what? How can we know and respect anger for the powerful emotion it is and yet not be driven by it, consciously, or even more damaging, without awareness? What is the antidote to anger?

The story of Jesus driving the money changers from the temple is memorable in part because it's one of the few stories in which Jesus is visibly angry. He expresses his anger dramatically, even violently. Not all versions of the story say, as John's version does, that he made a whip of cords to drive the money changers out, but the consensus is that he was really mad and that one way or another he threw them out — all those that he believed were desecrating the house of God.

Why Jesus thought the presence of those buying and selling in the temple was an offense to God is a fascinating question, one of considerable debate. Jesus consistently opposed any practice that denied people access to God. The temple practice of selling animals for sacrifice meant that only those who could afford the price of an animal were able to participate in those ritual offerings that were, nonetheless, required by religious law. He was consistently critical of those in religious authority for their tight control of spiritual practice and for exacting often crushing religious taxes on those already oppressed by the Roman authorities.

By the time the author, John, gets around to crafting his gospel, probably sixty years after Jesus died, the lines between the followers of Jesus and other Jews are pretty well drawn. John could refer to the religious authorities in this story as Jews, as if that somehow distinguished them from Jesus and his followers, who were, of course, also Jewish. But that simply shows how in just a few years this amazing, troubling story of Jesus' anger became a symbolic story, a sign of the conflict between the ways of God and those of corrupt religious leaders. Jesus' words and actions remind us that there are some things worth getting angry about, and yes, that God gets angry at some of the things we humans are capable of doing to one another.

Still, it's striking how rarely Jesus responds in anger to what he sees and experiences. There are only two other stories in the gospels of Jesus getting visibly angry. In one, on a day when Jesus is hungry, he curses a tree that has no fruit on it. By the next day when he and the disciples pass by again, the tree has shriveled and died.

I'm not sure what to make of that one.

The second story also takes place in the temple, this time on the sabbath. Before Jesus heals a man with a withered hand, his reputation as a healer and troublemaker for the authorities is already established. He looks around and realizes that the Pharisees are watching him like a hawk to see if he will dare break the rules of sabbath and heal the wounded man. Jesus is quietly furious at their hardness of heart, a hardness that keeps them from seeing how healing a wounded man is precisely the kind of act God would rejoice in, especially on the sabbath. "Humankind is not made for the sabbath," he tells the Pharisees, "but the sabbath for humankind." "Hold out your hand," he instructs the wounded man and he heals him. There are some things worth getting angry about. Withholding compassion to another in the name of God is, in Jesus' view, one of them.

Again, these stories are the exception, not the rule, of Jesus' life, and even they are muted in their effect. After healing the wounded man, Jesus walks away, refusing to engage the Pharisees further. After cleansing the temple, Jesus doesn't start an insurrection. He goes back to his twelve core disciples and prepares them for his suffering and death. Whatever meaning we are to take away from the cleansing of the temple, it isn't that anger and violence are the means God uses to transform the world.

In fact, the opposite is true. Jesus refuses to engage the powers of the world with the tools of power. His power is of love and forgiveness. That's it. No vengeance, no retribution, no demands

— simply love. "Hatred never ceases by hatred," the Buddha taught, "but by love alone is healed."[1] Jesus certainly lived that truth. We can say the same about how he dealt with anger. "Anger never ceases by anger, but by love alone is healed."

In a recent review of Gary Willis' book, *What Jesus Meant*, the reviewer, Jon Meacham, has this to say: "Jesus' essential message was that we are to love one another totally and unconditionally — a message fundamentally at odds with the impulses of those living in a fallen world." As one who lived in this fallen world, Jesus was not above anger. But anger is neither the message nor the medium of his life. Love is. "One cannot engage Jesus," writes Meacham, "without seeing there is no life without love."[2]

Back to the movie: In *Crash* there are stunning examples of love overcoming anger. The love is not a response to anger, but is rather an experience that transforms those touched by it and it washes some of their anger away. The same police officer who had sexually molested the African-American woman is the first to appear on the scene of an accident that trapped her in a car about to explode. When she realizes who he is, she screams and tries to push him away. In the moment when her life hangs in the balance, he perseveres and promises that he will not hurt her. As he works to pull her out of the car, they share a moment of tenderness, and he frees her just as the car bursts into flames. That experience of love changes them both. Like the anger they have carried, the love begins to spread into other realms of their life.

The Persian man who believed that a locksmith was responsible for a robbery that destroyed his store, goes off in a rage — with his gun — to hunt him down. At the precise moment his fury drives him to pull the trigger, the locksmith's little girl runs from the house and jumps into her father's arms. All are frozen in the horror of an innocent little girl being shot, until it becomes miraculously clear that she isn't hurt. Unbeknownst to him, the only bullets the Persian man had, thanks to his own daughter, were blanks. Spared from murdering a child, the Persian man visibly softens and his anger leaves him. He throws the gun away.

The wife of the district attorney falls down the stairs and sprains her foot. No one among her friends and family is available to help.

She can't reach her husband; her best friend is too busy getting a massage. But her housekeeper, a woman she has often verbally abused, finds her, takes her to the hospital and back again, and cares for her. The woman is overwhelmed by such love, and the love opens her heart. She is able to offer love, once again, to her husband.

Finally, the African-American thief makes the mistake of his life and attempts to steal the car of the African-American television director. Their lives collide just as the director can no longer contain his rage. He takes the gun from the thief and brandishes it boldly in front of several white police officers who now have every justification to kill him. Then one of the policemen recognizes him as the one unjustly stopped on the road, and he intervenes, saving the director's life, and unwittingly, that of the thief hiding in the front seat. Witnessing such courageous kindness from a white man on behalf of a black man changes the thief, and he goes off to commit an equally courageous act of love later on.

Anger is a powerful emotion, one that can be channeled in the service of good, but it's risky and the costs are high. There is plenty in the world to be angry about, justifiably so, and plenty that we get angry about whether we're justified or not. Some of us are better at expressing anger than others, but I don't know if how we express anger matters as much as how we experience and share love. Love is anger's only antidote. Love is what frees us to live.

The next time you find yourself really angry, you might take stock to consider how anger affects you. Then ask yourself: How can you love your way out of the anger you feel? How might the love of others and the love of God free you to let some of the anger go? And when you have a chance to be kind, generous, and loving to another — do it. Your act of love may be the needed antidote to someone else's anger, breaking the cycle of rage that you aren't even aware exists, sparing others untold pain. "Anger never ceases by anger, but by love alone is healed."

1. Quoted by Jack Kornfield in *The Art of Forgiveness, Lovingkindness, and Peace* (New York: Bantam Books, 2001), p. 5.

2. Jon Meacham "The Radical," in *The New York Times Book Review*, March 12, 2006, p. 28.

Lenten Season
John 6:4-14

Gathering Up The Fragments

*Now the Passover, the festival of the Jews, was near.
When he looked up and saw a large crowd coming toward him, Jesus said to Philip, "Where are we to buy
bread for these people to eat?" He said this to test him,
for he himself knew what he was going to do. Philip
answered him, "Six months' wages would not buy
enough bread for each of them to get a little." One of
his disciples, Andrew, Simon Peter's brother, said to
him, "There is a boy here who has five barley loaves
and two fish. But what are they among so many
people?" Jesus said, "Make the people sit down." Now
there was a great deal of grass in the place; so they sat
down, about five thousand in all. Then Jesus took the
loaves, and when he had given thanks, he distributed
them to those who were seated; so also the fish, as much
as they wanted. When they were satisfied, he told his
disciples, "Gather up the fragments left over, so that
nothing may be lost." So they gathered them up, and
from the fragments of the five barley loaves, left by those
who had eaten, they filled twelve baskets. When the
people saw the sign that he had done, they began to
say, "This is indeed the prophet who is to come into the
world."*   — John 6:4-14

When I think about or describe my life in terms of fragmentation, it isn't a positive assessment. Fragments of life can feel like
shards of glass. To live a fragmented life implies a lack of wholeness, a casting about from one thing to the next without a sense of
integration or forward movement. In all honesty, my life often feels
that way — fragmented, scattered in pieces that seem to require
attention and energy but, frankly, don't hang together very well.

To make matters worse, I am hopelessly drawn to the idea of living an undivided life — one of simplicity and grace.

Given my bias against fragmentation, when I read Jesus' words — "Gather up the fragments, so that nothing may be lost" — they caught me by surprise. All week I have felt both comforted and challenged by this imperative to gather up the fragments of my life. The comfort lies in the fact that if Jesus wants them gathered up, the fragments may, indeed, be worth something. The challenge lies in how to go about it. Like Humpty Dumpty, some things can't be put back together when they've been broken.

Then again, Jesus didn't say, "Put the fragments back together." He said, "Gather the fragments, so that none may be lost."

So I've been on a bit of a scavenger hunt this week, gathering the pieces of my life. I've paid attention to my dreams more than usual, not trying to interpret but simply remember them, gathering them up when I wake in the morning. I've noted my thoughts and feelings, not assuming that they're accurate reflections of reality, but gathering them, nonetheless. I've paid attention to my convictions, hopes, and concerns. I've taken stock of my commitments, the roles and responsibilities that define my life, the things I do by force of habit, the things I wish I had time for but don't, the relationships that come easily, and the ones that cost me.

In the gathering, I noticed that on occasion it would occur to me to do something with a particular fragment. I decided to act on what came to me, without overthinking it, as my spiritual practice for the week. I sent my father flowers for his birthday. I cleaned my desk. I attended a rally in St. Paul. I said good-bye to a friend who is dying. I walked the dog, did laundry, tried to be present to my family, came to work, and chipped away at the mountain of tasks waiting for me. And I dared to believe — perhaps the biggest act of faith of all — that what I have and can do is, by the grace of God, enough.

If the story of the loaves and fishes is true — and it is for me the miracle story that rings the most true — it teaches that God chooses to work miracles with what we offer. By itself what we offer is never enough: You know as well as I that five loaves of bread and a few fish will not feed five thousand people. But God takes what we offer to make miracles. It happens all the time. We give a little and that little bit becomes part of something bigger. The little bits, the scraps left over, the fragmented pieces that embarrass us, can move mountains sometimes. I don't know how it works; I only know that sometimes, when we give what we have, it does.

This notion of God taking what we offer to create a miracle doesn't mean much when we're satisfied with our efforts, confident that what we have to offer is what's needed. If the disciples had had enough food to feed the multitudes, that would have been an amazing, wonderful story but not one in need of a miracle. They didn't have enough and they knew it. All they had was what a young boy had offered up, hardly worth mentioning, really, given how many hungry mouths there were to feed. It's for those times when we know the gap between what we can offer and what's needed that the miracle of the loaves speaks to us.

Its message is simply this: Don't be afraid to give when you know that what you have to give isn't enough. Don't be afraid to offer what you have when the offering embarrasses you in its insignificance. Let the offering be what it is, and put yourself in the place of grace.

The writer, Anne Lamott, tells the story of starting a Sunday school in her church. "I didn't mean to start a Sunday school, and did not have a speck of confidence that I could do so ... I do not particularly like large groups of children, which is to say, more than two at a time, and I could not bear to miss any of the regular service, with which Sunday school would be concurrent. There was one more problem: There weren't any kids, except my son, Sam."[1]

She felt the tug to start something because it was right and because her son needed it. She recruited a friend, and with no guidance, support, or understanding, they began. It was predictably rocky at first, but soon they managed to attract eleven children: four black, four white, two Mexican, and one Asian — reflecting the makeup of their church. The work was good but a lot harder than she imagined: "Some of the kids were needy and vulnerable

131

and depressed ... some were wild. We didn't exclude anyone, because Jesus didn't," she writes. "On bad days I could not imagine what he had been thinking."[2] They kept lurching forward.

The crisis point came when all the original teachers, including Lamott, were on the verge of burnout and no one stepped up to help. Conflict erupted in the church along racial lines, as the all-white teachers tried to convince the parents of color to share responsibility, without sounding resentful or racist, or both. Lamott had some terrible phone conversations that ended up with her saying things like, "Why don't more of you black people help us with the kids?" and the black parents responding with very loud silences on the other end. But to their credit as a community, they hung in with each other, and slowly things got better. "Time and showing up," Lamott writes, "turn most messes into compost, and I have noticed this especially at my church."[3] Six years later this small, inner-city congregation has a dozen volunteers, a paid director, as many as thirty kids, a youth group of six or seven, and several babies.

While chaperoning the youth group on a beach outing, Lamott marveled at how her dream had come to life. It had cost a lot: "all the times we teachers had to ask for help, and had plugged away without enough resources, without knowing how, or whether we were going to manage. It had taken much more letting go and trusting that we felt capable of."[4] I think that from the inside, that's what a loaves and fishes miracle feels like: offering what you have knowing full well it's not enough, persevering in the offering, waiting for others to do the same, and trusting — never knowing for sure — that with God's help it will be enough.

The business writer, Jim Collins, speaks of this same loaves-and-fishes phenomenon in secular language. In his studies of what distinguishes a good organization from a great one, he likens the process of moving from good to great to turning an enormous flywheel — a massive metal disk mounted horizontally on an axle, thirty feet in diameter, two feet thick, and weighing 5,000 pounds. "Imagine that your task," he writes, "is to get the flywheel rotating on the axle as fast and as long as possible. So with great effort, you push, getting the flywheel to move ever so slowly. After two hours of persistent effort, you get the flywheel to complete one entire turn. You keep pushing and the flywheel begins to move a bit faster, until at last, the second rotation. You keep pushing in a consistent direction: Three turns ... four ... five ... six. The flywheel gradually builds up speed ... seven ... eight ... nine ... it builds momentum ... twenty ... thirty ... one hundred."[5]

Then at some point, you reach a breakthrough. Momentum kicks in, hurling the flywheel forward, turn after turn. You're not pushing any harder, but the flywheel goes faster, compounding your investment of earlier work. "Now if someone were to stop and ask you," Collins writes, "what was the one big push that caused this thing to move so fast? You wouldn't be able to answer; it's a nonsensical question. Was it the first push ... the second ... the hundredth? No it was all of them together in an overall accumulation of effort."[6] Each push is important, given the momentum that when it finally happens feel like grace. From the outside looks like it's easy, like a miracle, because no one sees the loneliness of one isolated push. But when that push is offered steadily, consistently, in full awareness of both its insignificance and its supreme importance, then true greatness is possible.

The reason Jesus wants us to gather up the fragments of our lives is because each one of the fragments is important. Gathered up, the fragments become available to us and available to God. Each one could help feed someone. Each one could be part of a larger effort of goodness unleashed in the world. We don't know that as we gather our fragments because to us they feel so insignificant. What if what we gather and hold before the light of God is what God needs? "Wholeness," Parker Palmer writes, "does not mean perfection: it means embracing brokenness as an integral part of life."[7]

So why not gather up the fragments of your life, so that nothing may be lost? You needn't try to hold them together. Simply honor them for what they are. Then, should the invitation come, either from the outside or from a tug on the shirtsleeve of your heart, dare to offer the fragment you have, knowing full well that by itself it won't be enough. But it might be the precise gift that another person needs, the word to soothe an aching heart, the spin of the flywheel that turns the momentum forward. Jesus stands ready to take our offerings and make of them a feast. The miracle is his, but he can't do it without us.

1. Anne Lamott, *Plan B: Further Thoughts on Faith* (New York: Riverhead Books, 2005), p. 60.

2. *Ibid*, p. 68.

3. *Ibid*, p. 75.

4. *Ibid*, p. 77.

5. Jim Collins, *Good to Great* (New York: HarperBusiness, 2001), p. 164.

6. *Ibid*, p. 165.

7. Parker Palmer, *A Hidden Wholeness: The Journey Toward an Undivided Life* (San Francisco: Jossey-Bass, 2004), p. 5.

Palm Sunday, Year B
Mark 14:1—15:47

A Different Kind Of Power

*They went to a place called Gethsemane; and he said
to his disciples, "Sit here while I pray." He took with
him Peter and James and John, and began to be dis-
tressed and agitated. And he said to them, "I am deeply
grieved, even to death; remain here, and keep awake."
And going a little farther, he threw himself on the ground
and prayed that, if it were possible, the hour might pass
from him. He said, "Abba, Father, for all things are
possible; remove this cup from me; yet not what I want,
but what you want."* — Mark 14:32-36

Who doesn't want to live a successful life? What a gift it is,
when hard work pays off and we get what we want, when seren-
dipity is on our side and we see our dreams realized. There is great
satisfaction and power in success.

God speaks to us today of another kind of power known in
failure, when everything goes wrong, the worst of fears confront
us, and we have no choice but to live through what we want most
to avoid.

Who can deny the beauty of health? What a glorious thing it is
to enjoy our bodies when they are strong and resilient and to marvel at athletes and dancers as they explore the outer limits of physical
capacity. We should all be amazed at what our bodies can do, as
does a child when first learning to walk or run. Yet God speaks
today of another kind of strength, revealed in weakness and suffering. It isn't a strength we relish to know firsthand, because it comes
at great cost. It is strength not in accomplishment but rather in
surrender.

Who doesn't long for joy, for happiness filling our hearts to
overflowing? Yet today reminds us of what we already know: that
in this life there is also sorrow and pain so deeply felt that our

hearts break from the weight of it. And it asks: What do we do then? Where do we turn then?

We are not wrong to strive for success, health, and joy. It's a good thing to avoid as best we can the anguish of failure, disease, and sorrow. Jesus encourages us to pray for our heart's desire and that God spare us from the times of trial. He prayed the same for himself, that the cup of sorrow might pass him by.

However, for reasons we will never understand, good does not always prevail and in every life there is hardship. Jesus accepted the cup as one he had to drink and that he could not spare his friends their suffering.

Why, then, do we commemorate the sad memory of Jesus' last week on earth and honor it with the significance of the word "holy"? Why indeed. It isn't because God prefers or requires suffering, but rather because of the power that comes to us from God in our suffering. Quite apart from the power of resurrection, which is a story all its own, there is redemption in suffering, when we allow darkness its hour and name it so.

Holy Week is the time for us to experience and remember this most important of Christian truths: that when the lights go out and darkness reigns, when we are no longer able to rely on our own power and strength, God is there with a different kind of power, a different kind of strength. We often resist it because it requires surrender. It is the power of endurance and the gift of peace that can bring us through our greatest trials. Our sorrow is not eliminated, but it is enfolded in God's love. Our suffering is not taken from us, but it is enveloped in God's light.

We cannot evoke this power on command, nor dare we judge ourselves for lacking it because it is a mystery and a gift. Yet in its presence we are awed beyond words.

One of the documentary films highlighted at a recent Sundance Film Festival was titled, *The Trials of Darryl Hunt*. It is the true story of a nineteen-year-old black man who in 1985 was convicted for the murder of a white woman in North Carolina. No physical evidence linked Hunt to the crime, and the case against him rested on the testimony of a former member of the Ku Klux Klan. From the beginning, Hunt maintained his innocence.

In 1989, the North Carolina Supreme Court ordered a new trial after the main witness recanted his statement. Hunt was offered a plea bargain that would have allowed him to be sentenced to time served, meaning that he would go free. But he refused to confess to something he had not done. Hunt was retried in 1990 and again convicted by an all-white jury and sentenced to life in prison.

In 1994, scientific advances allowed for DNA testing of evidence from the crime scene, and Hunt's DNA didn't match that of man who raped the murdered woman. But the prosecution insisted that there was more than one assailant and that Darryl Hunt could have still been the murderer. He remained in prison. Every effort to appeal the murder verdict failed; two governors refused to consider clemency.

In 2003, with Hunt in prison for almost two decades, the local paper published an eight-part series on the case revealing racism and negligence on the part of the prosecution. Shortly afterward, the State Bureau of Investigation ran the DNA from the crime scene against federal databases of convicted felons. A match was found, and another man eventually confessed to the murder, saying that he had acted alone. In 2004, Hunt was exonerated and set free.

The lessons we can learn from Darryl Hunt's story are many, but I tell you his story for one reason alone. I heard a radio interview with Darryl Hunt recently and what struck me was the gentleness in his voice. He spoke clearly of what life was like for him, both in and out of prison, but there was no malice or self-pity in his tone. After twenty years of imprisonment for a crime he didn't commit, I would have expected him to be angry and indignant. But he wasn't.

The year of his release, Hunt was invited to speak to the incoming class at Duke Law School. Among the many things he talked about was his faith in God. He said that while he will never get over what happened to him and there is no way to make up for the years he lost, God helped him to persevere while he was in prison and allows him to avoid bitterness now. "If God says he can forgive you, you can forgive others," he told the students. "I wanted to live. Bitterness and hatred can eat you up on the inside. I am at peace in my heart."

You know as well as I that such peace doesn't come easily, quickly, or without great cost. It comes only when we painstakingly learn to accept, on a daily basis, the things we wish we could change but can't, the hardships that don't go away, and the suffering we don't deserve. In the caldron of acceptance, God comes to us, enabling us to live without bitterness or rage and to persevere on the path we know is right, even when it's as hard as steel and there's no end in sight.

We begin this Holy Week with the procession of palms and telling the story of Jesus' suffering. We do so for consolation and assurance. When the worst of times happen to us, the events of this week remind us that we are not alone. God is with us offering strength in our weakness and the capacity to endure our trials, whatever they may be. While we would never wish for the kind of suffering through which such gifts are given; nonetheless, when the suffering comes, it's good to know that they are there. When life requires more than we have to give, God is there, loving us, giving us the courage to persevere, and offering us the peace of God that surpasses human understanding.

Easter Day, Year A
Acts 10:34-43
John 20:1-18

Trusting The Rope Will Hold

*Then Peter began to speak to them: "... You know the
message he sent to the people of Israel, preaching peace
by Jesus Christ — he is Lord of all ... he went about
doing good and healing all who were oppressed by the
devil, for God was with him ... They put him to death by
hanging him on a tree; but God raised him on the third
day...."*   — Acts 10:34a, 36a, 38b, 39b-40

*... She turned around and saw Jesus standing there, but
she did not know that it was Jesus. Jesus said to her,
"Woman, why are you weeping? Whom are you looking for?" Supposing him to be the gardener, she said to
him, "Sir if you have carried him away, tell me where
you have laid him, and I will take him away." Jesus
said to her, "Mary!" She turned and said to him in
Hebrew, "Rabbouni!" (which means Teacher). Jesus
said to her, "Do not hold on to me, because I have not
yet ascended to the Father. But go to my brothers and
say to them, "I am ascending to my Father and your
Father, to my God and your God."* — John 20:14-17

There is a world of difference between believing things *about*
Jesus and believing *in* Jesus.

The two are related: you can't believe in Jesus if you don't
hold certain convictions about him. You can't know him without
knowing about him. The difference is like the difference between
reading about love and falling in love, between studying the proper
technique for rock climbing versus knowing what it's like to lean
back in mid-air, entrusting your life to the rope around your waist
and the person beneath you.

Nonetheless, faith in Jesus begins by learning about him. Learning about him is no easy task, particularly now, when distortions and misperceptions about him abound. The caricatures of Jesus in culture are among the greatest obstacles to believing in him — or worse, they can lead to belief in a false Jesus. But I wonder if it isn't easier to hold onto caricatures we reject as a means of avoiding knowing him as he is and risking a relationship that might change us.

This is what I know about Jesus. He was born in Palestine during the reign of Herod the Great. He grew up in the town of Nazareth. He emerged as a public figure in his early thirties, rising out of the movement begun by the John the Baptist, he had a ministry of healing and teaching that lasted about three years, focused primarily in the region of Galilee. He made the fateful decision, however, to bring his message to Jerusalem, the center of religious and political power. There he openly challenged the religious leaders of his people, which did not sit well with them. He also aroused suspicions of the Roman authorities and that led to his crucifixion, a form of death they reserved for insurrectionists and escaped slaves.

It's impossible to understand Jesus without placing him in the tradition of the spiritual prophets of ancient Judaism. These were people who had a strong sense of a spiritual realm that informs and gives meaning to human existence. Jesus was exceptionally connected to and empowered by this spiritual realm, and he used his connection to heal people and teach them how to live. He lived to help people know God as he knew God. As we heard his disciple, Peter, say about him, "Jesus *went around doing good*."

The world religions scholar, Huston Smith, describes Jesus this way:

> *Circulating easily among ordinary people and social misfits, healing them, counseling them, helping them out of chasms of despair, Jesus went around doing good. People tend to dislike being interrupted, but it was impossible to interrupt Jesus because he simply dealt with*

what was at hand. He did so with such single-mindedness and effectiveness that those who were with him found their estimate of him persistently modulating to a new key. They found themselves thinking that if divine goodness were to manifest itself in human form, this is how it would behave.[1]

Jesus was also an extraordinarily vivid teacher. "Jesus talks of camels that squeeze their humps through needles' eyes," Huston Smith writes. "His characters go around with timbers protruding from their eyes while they look for tiny specks in the eyes of others and of people whose outer lives are stately mansions while their inner lives stink of decaying corpses." His teaching style was invitational. "Instead of telling people what to do or believe," Smith writes, "he invited them to *see* things differently, confident that if they did so, their behavior would change."[2]

Jesus' core message is simple, summarized in a few, often-repeated phrases: "Love your neighbor as yourself." "Love your enemies." "Blessed are the poor." "Forgive not seven times, but seventy times seven." "Come unto me all you that labor and are heavy laden and I will give you rest." "You shall know the truth and the truth shall set you free."

Most of the time Jesus told stories: of buried treasure, lost coins, and sowers in the field; of a good Samaritan (which would be like us telling a story today about a *good* terrorist), and of a man who had two sons. More than anything Jesus wanted people to believe two important facts of life: God's overwhelming love for us and of our need to accept that love and let it flow through us.

Jesus lived in such a way that people believed him when he spoke of God's love, for he himself loved freely. His heart went out to all people, no matter if they were rich or poor, young or old, saints or sinners. He knew that everyone has a need to belong and he encouraged those who had the means to invite the poor, the crippled, the lame, and the blind to their tables. He loved children and he hated injustice for what it did to the most vulnerable people. He also hated hypocrisy, for what it did to the human soul.[3]

141

This is who Jesus was when he lived on this earth. I want you to know these things about him and more, all that helps you understand why our ancestors began to speak of him as the one in whom the fullness of God was pleased to dwell, how they came to the extraordinary conclusion that in Jesus we see not only what it means to be fully human, but also God.

In the words of Saint Paul:

> *Though he was in the form of God, he did not regard equality with God as something to be exploited, but emptied himself, taking the form of a slave, being born in human likeness. And being found in human form, he humbled himself and became obedient to the point of death — even death on the cross.*
>
> — Philippians 2:5-11

From the gospel of John:

> *In the beginning was the Word, and the Word was with God, and the Word was God. All things came into being through him, and without him not one thing came into being. What has come into being in him was life, and that life was the light of all people ... He was in the world, and the world came into being through him, yet the world did not know him. He came to his own people, and his own people did not accept him. But to all who received him, who believed in his name, he gave power to become children of God. The Word became flesh and dwelt among us, and we have seen his glory, the glory of a father's only son, full of grace and truth.*
>
> — John 1:1, 3-4, 10-12, 14

These are beautiful and essential Christian teachings. But you know, if that's all that the church did — teach about Jesus and pass beliefs about him down from one generation to the next — it wouldn't be enough. As important as these teachings are, quite bluntly, it wouldn't be worth your time and effort to come to church, nor mine, if learning about him were all we were here to do, if in

142

the process of learning about Jesus we didn't come to believe in him in a way that makes a difference in how we live.

Believing in Jesus is not easy. If you struggle with your belief in him, don't imagine that you're alone. Or if you don't struggle because you've already decided that you can't believe in him, or don't want to, don't imagine that somehow sets you apart from the rest of us.

The writer, Kathleen Norris, describes her struggle with Jesus this way: "When I first began to attend church services as an adult, I found it ironic that it was the language about Jesus, meant to be the most inviting, that made me feel the most left out ... I felt a void at the center of things. My Christianity seemed to be missing its center." I can't tell you how many people have said something like that to me, that it would be easier to be Christian if we didn't talk about Jesus all the time.

When Kathleen Norris confessed her feelings about Jesus to a monk, he reassured her by saying, "Oh, most of us feel that way at one time or another. Jesus is the hardest part of the religion to grasp, to keep alive."[4] Norris, like most of us, came around to Jesus gradually. "I caught glimpses of him," she writes. "One day in church I heard the lines, 'Do this in memory of me,' as if for the first time, as a plea from a man about to die. In my reading I encountered a thirteenth-century housewife who told of Christ appearing to her asking, 'Why have you abandoned me, who never abandoned thee?' " And then friends began to tell her how much they were inspired by her love of Christ. "I didn't think I had any," she wrote, "but I began to realize that the joke might be on me."[5]

What does it look like to believe in Jesus? I think we catch glimpses of him, too, and like Mary at the tomb, we don't recognize him, at first. Sometimes we don't recognize him at all. But other times, deep inside, we hear him call our names: Mary — Mariann — Frank — Carole — Steve. In that moment, we feel his presence and love.

One of the first times I consciously heard his voice was when I was in my early twenties. It was during a time when everyday life asked of me something I didn't know how to do. I woke up every morning anxious and afraid. One day, railing against my life as I took a walk, I asked, "Is it always going to be like this?" I didn't think of my question as a prayer, but it must have been, because the answer came immediately: "Yes." Then I heard: "But I will be with you." Imagine that. I wasn't alone.

Believing in him is also like leaning into thin air, trusting that a rope will hold. It involves letting go. When I imagine what it will be like to die, I think of leaning back, letting go, and trusting that God will be there to catch me. Believing in Jesus now involves practicing in small ways of leaning back and letting go as I live.

Believing in Jesus involves accepting change. Resurrection is about change. To believe in resurrection is to trust that we can have another chance, a fresh start. More than that: to believe in resurrection is to trust that no matter how bad things get, no matter how stark the failure or disappointment or grief, God can raise new life in us.

Let me suggest two concrete ways to practice believing in Jesus. The first: Whenever life gets hard, really hard, and you don't know if you can face what it is that life is asking of you, or to let go of, or to change, *lean into the pain*. Don't run away. Lean into it, and open yourself to the grace of Christ in that place. I promise you that he will meet you there. You can trust that the rope will hold, the ground beneath you is firm, and that you are not alone.

Second, whenever you are at a crossroads, when you have a decision to make and you aren't sure what to do, pay attention to what inspires you, makes your heart beat faster, and gives you joy. Follow your inspiration, and live by it, and I promise you that Jesus will meet you there. That doesn't mean that you'll succeed in living your inspiration: You will often fail, but so what? Whether we succeed or fail matters far less than the choice to live according to what inspires us. Failure is never the final word.

Inspiration takes many forms, some dramatic to help us through big decisions, and some rather ordinary. A student once asked Peter Gomes, the chaplain at Harvard, what inspired him. No one was more surprised than Gomes himself by his answer. What inspired him, he said, was the beginning of each new day. "When I wake up each morning, I rejoice that I've been given a chance to start over. When I get up in the middle of the night, as I do from time to time, and stumble on my way to a private mission and hurt my toe, I don't swear. I say, 'Thank God I'm still alive to feel this!' For I know that when morning comes, I have a chance to start over."[6]

That is what today is for us, too: a new day, a fresh start, with the assurance of God's presence with us, and through us, in the world. We can make of it what we choose. We can go it alone if that's our wish. But if we choose to believe in him, Christ can be our companion and friend, our courage and inspiration. It's not a decision that Christians make once and are done with. It's a daily choice, and some days are easier than others. But as we invite him, day by day he comes and makes his home in us. He calls us by name. He is our strength, our peace, and our path.

1. Huston Smith *The Soul of Christianity* (San Francisco: HarperSanFrancisco, 2005), p. 48.

2. *Ibid*, p. 51.

3. This is a summary of Smith's description as found in *The Soul of Christianity.* I am indebted to Smith for this sermon's inspiration.

4. Kathleen Norris, *Amazing Grace* (New York: Riverhead Books, 1998), pp. 161-162.

5. *Ibid,* p. 161.

6. Peter Gomes, "Starting Over," in *Strength for the Journey* (San Francisco: HarperSanFrancisco, 2003), p. 258.

Easter Day, Year A
Matthew 28:1-10 (alternative reading)

Easter Imperatives

Almighty God, by the glorious resurrection of your Son Jesus Christ, you have broken the power of death and brought life and immortality to life. Help us to face the future with courage and assurance, knowing that nothing in life or death can ever part us from your love....
— prayer for Easter Day

After the sabbath, as the first day of the week was dawning, Mary Magdalene and the other Mary went to see the tomb. And suddenly there was a great earthquake; for an angel of the Lord, descending from heaven, came and rolled back the stone and sat on it. His appearance was like lightning, and his clothing white as snow. For fear of him the guards shook and became like dead men. But the angel said to the woman, "Do not be afraid; I know that you are looking for Jesus who was crucified. He is not here; for he has been raised, as he said. Come, see the place where he lay. Then go quickly and tell his disciples, 'He has been raised from the dead, and indeed he is going ahead of you to Galilee; there you will see him.' This is my message for you." So they left the tomb quickly with fear and great joy, and ran to tell his disciples. Suddenly Jesus met them and said, "Greetings!" And they came to him, took hold of his feet, and worshiped him. Then Jesus said to them, "Do not be afraid; go and tell my brothers to go to Galilee; there they will see me." — Matthew 28:1-10

The poet, Emily Dickinson, a woman of passionate faith and fierce independence, once told a friend that "consider the lilies" was the only commandment she every obeyed. Inspired by Dickinson, another poet, Kathleen Norris, combed through the New

147

Testament to find other hidden commandments of Jesus. This is what she found and recorded in a poem titled, "Imperatives":

> *Look at the birds*
> *Consider the lilies*
> *Drink ye all of it*
> *Ask*
> *Seek*
> *Knock*
> *Enter by the narrow door*
> *Do not be anxious*
> *Judge not; do not give dogs what is holy*
> *Go; be it done for you*
> *Do not be afraid*
> *Maiden, arise*
> *Young man, I say, arise*
> *Stretch out your hand*
> *Stand up, be still*
> *Rise, let us be going*
> *Love*
> *Forgive*
> *Remember me*[1]

There is an imperative on Easter morning as well, calling us to rise and face a new day. This Easter imperative comes not as a command from a drill sergeant wanting to whip us into shape, but rather as an invitation from one who knows and loves us. Can you hear it? What might your Easter imperative be? Is this the day for you to rise up and walk or to consider the lilies and look at the birds with new eyes? Is this the day for you to allow God's forgiveness to wash over you or to offer forgiveness to another? Is this the first day of a new life for you? Might you walk out of church a different person, transformed by the mercy and love of God?

No one can tell another what his or her Easter imperative is. It must be heard and responded to from within. But if I were to wager a guess, based on what the scriptures say and what seems to be in the air around here these days, I would say that your imperative, and mine, has to do with letting go of whatever is holding us back from living our lives with confidence, courage, and joy. I would say that it has to do with acceptance, accepting the assurance we need to live boldly, love lavishly, and forgive generously. I would say that it has to do with letting go of fear. "Do not be afraid," the angel said to the women gathered at the tomb. Moments later, Jesus said the same thing, "Do not be afraid." Objectively speaking, it wasn't as if there was nothing to fear. But the Easter imperative is one of courage: They didn't have to *live* in fear anymore.

Jesus is not asking us to pretend that there is nothing to fear — that would be delusional. There is so much to inspire fear in this world that were we to consider each thing we might not have courage to get out of bed in the morning. There are so many things that bring us face-to-face with uncertainty and limitations and sorrow. There is so much sorrow. We, of all people, are not to avert our gaze.

While the sorrow of our time, of this particular week, has its own distinctive power to knock the breath out of us, sorrow itself is not new. We know this, even as we grieve for the family of the latest Minnesotan to be killed in a war the nation would rather forget, and for the people of Red Lake, caught in the double grief of loss and media frenzy. We know, even as we bring our own struggles, tribulations, and worries with us, the struggles and tribulations and worries are not new. Indeed, one of the greatest burdens for those of us who call ourselves Christians is this: Given the love and mercy and power of God, why does so little in the world seem to change?

But you see, asking what changes in resurrection isn't the right question. The question is not what, but who — who changes and how? In the words of Harvard chaplain, Peter Gomes:

> *The heart and burden of the Easter story is not that the world changed, but that ordinary men and women were changed from the ordinary to the extraordinary. Jesus' disciples were changed, and thus was their attitude toward the world. They were no longer afraid of their shadows, frightened, or fearful of death. They were no*

149

longer in awe of people who had power over them. Read about those apostles in the New Testament; read about what happens to them, about how they lived their lives, how they faced the world, how they astonished everyone who knew them before the resurrection. Can these be the same people who never understood one of Jesus' parables, who were always late, who were never in the right place at the right time, who denied him, who shivered at the foot of the cross, who ran into the darkness, and who didn't even believe the good news when they first heard it? Could it be these same people who were now turning the world upside down?[2]

That's the power of an Easter imperative — it changes us from within. It changes us from the people we are to the people we know we long to be, the people we were born to be. It changes us from people driven by anxiety and worry and self-protection to people of great generosity and love and courage. It changes us from people defined by our problems and limitations to people transformed and liberated by them. Resurrection doesn't change the world — resurrection changes *us* and how we live. Then, through us, the world is changed, one loving, generous, courageous step at a time.

How does this happen? How are we changed by the Easter imperative? The most honest answer: "I don't know." Logic cannot be our guide in resurrection. I've been thinking all week of a wonderful line from the movie, *Shakespeare in Love*, when the owner of a bankrupt theater tries to explain to his creditors what the theater is like: "The natural condition," he says, "is one of insurmountable obstacles on the road to imminent disaster." "What can be done about it?" his creditor asks. "Nothing," he replies. "It all turns out well." "How?" "I don't know. It's a mystery."

Resurrection is a mystery, lifting us beyond our insurmountable obstacles and sparing us from imminent disasters. We can't define, predict, or control it, for resurrection is God's way, God's capacity to transform us. All I can say is that when it happens, we ought not to fight it, question too much, or analyze it to death. We should simply live the resurrection that comes to us for the grace and the mystery that it is.

There is one thing we can do, however. We can, in the words of Wendell Berry, *practice resurrection.* We can learn the steps, practicing a new way of being ourselves. "It's not so terrible," writes Kathleen Norris in another poem, "It's like the piano lessons you love and hate. You know how you want the music to sound, but you have to practice, half in tears."[3]

Yet we do not practice resurrection alone. The Archbishop of Canterbury, Rowan Williams, describes the way of resurrection as learning to dance, taught by one who already knows the steps. He tells the story of a young teacher who taught severely mentally and physically handicapped people in Australia, their accomplishment featured in a televised performance from the Sydney Opera House. The archbishop confessed that he first watched their performance prepared to feel moved in a patronizing sort of way, only to be humbled by the magnitude of their grace and beauty. He described how the teacher taught her students to value and admire their bodies, showing them by example how to circle their arms and move their hands. That's how dancing is taught — by example and mirroring.

> *Listen to the invitation. Sit down, all you handicapped, lumpish, empty, afraid, and start to feel that you too are rooted in a firm, rich earth. Opposite you is someone who, it seems, doesn't need to learn. Dancing is natural to him. So he begins: he stretches out his arms, wide as he can. And so do you. Then he rises up, arms to the sky. And so do you. Then he takes your hand and swings you loose and leaves you to improvise to the music — on your own, then combining with others ... He dances so that you will dance. He shows you what beauty is ... He repeats over and over his central gesture — arms flung wide, then palms carried upward as he stands on the earth, carrying you, embracing you.*[4]

We do not practice resurrection alone. The one who gives us the imperative is right there in front of us, showing us the steps, teaching us the way, reminding us as we stumble and fall that we are lovely and beloved, and through the mysterious power of resurrection, we can be transformed. Look at the birds. Consider the lilies. Do not be anxious. Do not be afraid. Rise, love, forgive, remember, and be you transformed.

---

1. Kathleen Norris, "Imperatives," in *Little Girls in Church* (Pittsburgh: University of Pittsburgh Press, 1995), p. 62.

2. Peter Gomes, *Strength for the Journey: A New Collection of Sermons* (San Francisco: HarperSanFrancisco, 2003), p. 261.

3. *Op cit*, Norris, "The Age of Reason," p. 28.

4. Rowan Williams, "My Dancing Day," in *A Ray of Darkness* (Cambridge: Cowley Publications, 1995), pp. 62-63.

The Ascension Of Our Lord or
Memorial Day
Ephesians 1:15-23
Luke 24:49-53

Jesus Doesn't Divide The World

I pray that the God of our Lord Jesus Christ, the Father of glory, may give you a spirit of wisdom and revelation as you come to know him, so that, with the eyes of your heart enlightened, you may know what is the hope to which he has called you....
— Ephesians 1:17-18

[Jesus said to his disciples,] "And see, I am sending upon you what my Father promised; so stay here in the city until you have been clothed with power from on high." Then he led them as far as Bethany, and, lifting up his hands, he blessed them. While he was blessing them, he withdrew from them and was carried up into heaven. And they worshiped him, and returned to Jerusalem with great joy; and they were continually in the temple blessing God. — Luke 24:49-53

Tony Hendra, a British comedian, once tried to describe the function of satire — humor told at the expense of another person, often with fierce ridicule and contempt — to his spiritual mentor, a gentle Benedictine monk named Father Joe. "Satire," he explained, "is a weapon the powerless have against the powerful. Or the poor against the rich. Or the young against the old." "Satire always divides people up into two groups?" Father Joe asked. "Yes." "Is that a good thing?"

"It's the way the world works, Father Joe. People think in teams. We're good; you're evil; we're smart; you're dumb. Most humor works that way, even the most basic jokes. The English tell Irish jokes. Americans tell Polish jokes, because the Poles have been stereotyped as stupid."

153

"Tell me a Polish joke," Father Joe said. "Okay," Tony replied. "What has an IQ of 212?" "I don't know, dear." "Warsaw." Father Joe gazed up expectantly. "Is there a joke coming?" "That's it. The entire city of Warsaw has a combined IQ of 212." "Oh, but the Poles are a rather sensitive people," Father Joe protested. "Tragic and poetic and long-suffering. Look at Chopin — or the Holy Father." "Okay Chopin and John Paul the Second are not Polish jokes. But the dynamic holds for jokes about politicians, blondes, or the French." Father Joe looked puzzled. "To say people are stupid when they're not — isn't that a little cruel?"

He was silent for a moment. "You see, dear, I think there are two types of people in the world. Those who divide the world into two types of people, and those who don't."[1]

If you think about it, satire and war share the same premise. In war, as in satire, you must divide the world into two groups: your allies and your enemies, the good versus the evil, us against them. It's essential for soldiers in war to define their enemies and be prepared to kill them, something hard to do if they think about what they and their enemies have in common.

The war we are currently fighting in Iraq has created sharp divisions among us as a nation. We are clearly on teams: those who supported the war when we first invaded Iraq and those who didn't; those who still support the war (a number, if the pollsters are right, that is diminishing) and those who don't. We are divided according to those who now believe that the only way out of the quagmire we find ourselves in is to withdraw our troops and those who believe we can't walk away from the mess we've helped to create, or in the more positive language of our president, until the mission is complete.

On this Memorial Day weekend, I'd like to suggest another division between us as Americans: Those who are actually fighting this war and those of us who are not, or to broaden the lens, those who have family members and friends fighting in Iraq and those who don't. The actual number of Americans fighting is relatively small, certainly in comparison to past wars. During the Civil War, which was the inspiration for Memorial Day, or Decoration Day, as it was called then, over three million people fought and over 500,000 people died, a number if adjusted to the current population would be over ten million. Memorial Day began as a way to honor the dead, and everyone in the nation loved someone who had died in the war. Everyone paid a price. During the Second World War, the war often remembered at the most noble of American wars, sixteen million people served in the military and, of course, every American felt the impact of that war, with the rationing of food and other essentials and the redirecting of resources to pay for the war as we fought it.

In the current war, those of us who aren't fighting and don't have family members in the Middle East are asked to do very little in support. Moral support is appreciated, in the form of bumper stickers and the like. But we're not being asked to share the burden, although we certainly will in the future when the credit card bill comes. We're not asked to sacrifice now. There is no draft, no increase in taxes to pay for the war, no limiting of our consumption to direct supplies to the troops.

Those who are fighting in Iraq, in contrast, are asked to sacrifice everything. Over 2,400 soldiers and national guardsmen have lost their lives. Countless others have lost limbs, mobility, and brain function. Family members have lost loved ones — fathers, mothers, sons, daughters, spouses — gone forever.

Buried in the back of the *New York Times*, at least once — sometimes twice a week — there appears a small box with the heading, "Names of the Dead." Below that a brief statement, as in the one on May 25, 2006, which read: "The Department of Defense has identified 2,452 American service members who have died since the start of the Iraq war. It confirmed the deaths of the following Americans this week." And then the names:

> *Christoff, David, R, age 25, from Rossford, Ohio, Third*
> *   Marine Division*
> *Hermanson, Michael, age 21, from Fargo, North Da-*
> *   kota, Army National Guard*
> *Leusink, William, J, age 21, from Maurice, Iowa, Third*
> *   Marine Division*
> *Rameriz, Benito, age 21 from Edinburg, Texas, First*
> *   Marine Division[2]*

As you read the obituaries of those who have died in Iraq, the first thing that strikes you about them is their youth. It is always so in war: Young people do not plan and strategize wars, but they disproportionately fight and die in them. For one woman in central Wisconsin, the death that haunts her is that of a young man who enlisted and died right after high school. He had no time to make his mark on the world; his was, as yet, an unlived life.[3]

Some of our young fellow Americans enlist in the military with a fervent patriotism and desire to protect our country, particularly so after the attacks of September 11. Others — the majority — enlist because, frankly, they don't have a lot of options: their grades in high school weren't great; they didn't go to college; they live in depressed areas; they don't have marketable job skills; and they are in debt. Not all support the war, but many do. In fact, of those paying the greatest price for this war, the percentage supporting it is higher than of those who aren't. That shouldn't surprise us: They are risking their lives. Many are, in their minds, fighting a war of good versus evil, freedom against tyranny, America versus the terrorist threat, us versus them. The military is not, in general, a bad place for them. My sister pulled her life out of chaos by dedicating her life to the military, and one of her sons is currently doing the same. It is also true that our leaders feed and fuel their naiveté and immaturity. Many young men and women are fighting in Iraq because they believe that Saddam Hussein was responsible for the attacks on September 11.

"There are two types of people in the world. Those who divide the world into two types of people, and those who don't."

Toward the end of the Easter season there is, in the Christian calendar, a day called the Feast of the Ascension, that tells of Jesus' post-resurrection ascent into heaven, or perhaps better stated, the transition from being Jesus of Nazareth, rooted in one historical moment of time, to Jesus the Christ, available and present to all people in every time. Jesus of Nazareth died a political martyr. Jesus the Christ died to reconcile humanity to God. Jesus the Christ lives now in and for all of us, whether we acknowledge him or not, know him or not, believe in him or not. His ministry is one of love and reconciliation and forgiveness for every human being. To follow him means to accept the brokenness that lives in each one of us, to take our place in and among a broken yet glorious humanity, and to seek and serve Christ in all people. To follow him requires us to give up thinking in terms of us/them, good/evil. For we are all on the same team in his mind. We're all on the same side.

This is not a day to debate military policy. Nor is it a day for simplistic patriotism, on the assumption that we, as a nation, are always in the right in war. It is, foremost, a day to remember and to grieve the loss of those who died in war, the ones whose lives were cut off too soon, young men and women, subjected to the worst that human beings can do to one another.

From Minnesota, 35 have died. Some were married; most were single. Four had children. The youngest, a Marine, was 18; the oldest, an Army Reservist, was 44.[4]

Edward James Hogart, age twenty, from Shakopee, was the first Minnesotan to die in the war, in 2003. Robert Posivio, from Sherborn, was the latest Minnesotan to die. He had just returned to Iraq last month after recovering from injuries sustained in a previous attack. It was his third tour of duty. He was due to be discharged on July 28.

We have every reason to be in awe of these men and women. And every reason to question what we are asking them to do in our name.

1. Tony Hendra, *Father Joe: the Man Who Saved My Soul* (New York: Random House, 2004), p. 190.

2. "Names of the Dead," in *The New York Times,* May 25, 2006, p. A-8.

3. Heard on an interview on *National Public Radio*, May 26, 2006.

4. "Remembering Minnesotans Who Died in Iraq," in *The Minneapolis Star Tribune*, May 25, 2006.

The Day Of Pentecost, Year A
Acts 2:1-21
1 Corinthians 12:3b-13
John 7:37-39

A Force To Contend With

When the day of Pentecost had come, they were all to-gether in one place. And suddenly from heaven there came a sound like the rush of a violent wind, and it filled the entire house where they were sitting. Divided tongues, as of fire, appeared among them, and a tongue rested on each of them. All of them were filled with the Holy Spirit and began to speak in other languages, as the Spirit gave them ability. — Acts 2:1-4*

Now there are varieties of gifts, but the same Spirit; and there are varieties of services, but the same Lord; and there are varieties of activities, but it is the same God who activates all of them in everyone. To each is given the manifestation of the Spirit for the common good. — 1 Corinthians 12:4-7

As the scripture has said, "Out of the believer's heart shall flow rivers of living water." — John 7:38

If we wanted to encounter the Holy Spirit of God, where would we look? And how would we know that we are in the Spirit's presence?

In scripture, the Holy Spirit is often likened to the power of wind, blowing where it will, sometimes gently and at other times with tremendous force. The Spirit is also described as breath, the life force within each person. If those images are to be trusted, then our search for the Spirit must take us both deep within ourselves and far beyond, just as breath moves in and out of our bodies and wind travels freely across the planet.

159

The Spirit, like breath and wind, is a force to reckon with. As described in the book of Acts, the Spirit cares about the way we communicate with one another. Saint Paul tells us that the Spirit functions within us as a catalyst of sorts, freeing us to exercise our God-given gifts. At a recent confirmation service, the bishop prayed for over 100 people, asking that the Spirit might be released in them so that they might experience the power of God working through them.

It sounds good: "God working in us." But sometimes I wonder if, honestly, we'd prefer that God's Spirit leave us alone. Life is hard enough. What if, on top of everything, the Spirit's presence is disruptive and unsettling? What if the Spirit's intention is to take us where we aren't ready to go or ask us to do what we don't want to do?

I read a sermon this week by a preacher who lives in the Deep South. In that part of the country, the Feast of Pentecost almost always coincides with the beginning of hurricane season. Wind, therefore, is not a particularly reassuring image for the Spirit of God. Her descriptions of the hurricane force with which God had rearranged her life one particular summer reminded me of a passage in one of the Narnia tales by C. S. Lewis. You may remember that in the magical land of Narnia, God appears in the form of a great and mysterious lion named Aslan. One of the children who had stumbled into Narnia and encountered the lion wondered, "Is Aslan *safe*?" "Safe?" a resident of Narnia replied. "No, my dear, Aslan is not safe. But he is *good*."

Can it be that God's Spirit is at once unsafe, but good? I think so, in the sense that we will often experience the Holy Spirit as disruptive at first, even unwelcome, stirring things up in and around us. But that stirring up may be a necessary step in creating new possibilities. My southern preacher put it this way: "We are often trapped by life, by too many good things or too many bad things. Afraid to leave and afraid to stay, we move into survival mode. Pentecost marks the descent of the Holy Spirit of God — a spirit different from our own. It is the hurricane-like wind that, if we have the courage to conspire with it, will rearrange us into people who can be more than we are and do more than we do — not just for ourselves, but for others. It is the earth-shaking blast that affords us power to choose love instead of hate, acceptance over judgment."[1]

One place, then, to consider the Spirit's presence in your life and mine is where things are stirred up, shaken around, and unsettled. It may not feel very good right now, but the shaking and stirring may be exactly what we need for reasons beyond our knowing. Or it may be that what's swirling around us is not of God at all but is the raw material God has to work with, helping us to stretch and grow.

Yet it would be a mistake to stop and assume that the Spirit is only disruptive, its function only to shake us out of complacency. That's the wind part, when it blows with hurricane intensity. But then comes the breath part, that which lives deep within you and me. The breath part says to us, "In the midst of all that's swirling around you, be still. Go to that place inside where you find your core strength and goodness." This is the Spirit's gift when we feel overwhelmed or overcome by what's happening around us, when life conspires to disconnect us from our core truth and keeps us focused on the things that matter least in life rather than on what matters most.

So if you want to encounter the Holy Spirit in whatever ways work for you, find a way to connect with yourself at the deepest level of who you are. The Spirit of God, Jesus told his disciples, lies within you. The writer, Anne Lamott, in the speech she gives whenever asked to speak at commencement services, tells new graduates, "Your spiritual identity is something you feel best when you're not doing much — when you're in nature, when you're very quiet, or paradoxically, when you're listening to music. I know that you can feel the Spirit and hear it in the music you love, in the bass line, in the harmonies, in the silence between notes."[2] Contemplative Christians assure us that we can feel the Spirit if we simply pay attention to our breath — breathing in and out, allowing our minds to calm down so that we can listen from the core. That's where the Spirit lives and speaks most profoundly, at that core place, even as the winds howl.

How will we be able to recognize the Spirit's presence apart from our own, hear the Spirit's voice as distinctive from our own voice? That's not always easy, but the clues for me are when the Spirit speaks — if even "speaking" is the right way to describe it — in ways that get my attention, that counter my own perceptions in a way that points me toward God. It's the presence that counters my internal anxiety, for example, with an assurance that what I'm worried about will turn out all right. The Spirit allows me to listen to the hurricane around me with a bit of detachment and curiosity. What can I learn from this? How is God using this circumstance to teach me something important? The Spirit shifts my perception of another person or a situation, giving me the capacity to be kind when I am hurt, non-defensive when challenged, accepting when I'm disappointed, and forgiving when I would rather rehearse and refine my anger.

That leads me, my friends, to the last and most important place we can encounter the Holy Spirit: in relationship to one another, and in particular, again using the words of Anne Lamott, when we simply push up our sleeves and start helping. "Every spiritual tradition," she tells those graduating, "says that you must take care of the poor, that you can make a difference in the lives of those who are poor in spirit, worried, or who have given up hope. You can do what you can, what good people have always done: You bring thirsty people water, you share your food, you try to help the homeless find shelter, you stand up for the underdog."[3]

When we're willing to allow others their imperfections and simply offer to help, the Holy Spirit will meet us more than halfway. "We see the Spirit made visible," Lamott writes, "when people are kind to one another, especially when it's a really busy person like you, taking care of a needy, annoying, neurotic person, like you. In fact, that's often when we see the Spirit most brightly."[4]

So let the wind blow gently or fiercely all around you and pay attention for what the Spirit might be saying. Go deep within yourself, however you best get there, breathe and pay attention. Look around and offer whatever olive branch, word of kindness, or gesture of generosity you can to another and pay attention. Look at the beautiful children and their families who have come seeking baptism and the assurance that for all the dangers of the world, for all the ways that even God can be scary, that goodness will prevail. Pay attention to the ways you might be part of the blessing they seek. The Spirit is around, within and between us, a force to reckon with and God's greatest gift to those open to receive it.

---

1. "Hurricane Season," by Margaret Austin Smith, in *Preaching Through Holy Days and Holidays: Sermons That Work XI*, Roger Alling and David Schlafer, eds. (Harrisburg, Pennsylvania: Morehouse Publishing, 2003), p. 11.

2. Anne Lamott, "Let Us Commence," in *Plan B: Further Thoughts on Faith* (New York: Riverhead Books, 2005), p. 306.

3. *Ibid*, p. 307.

4. *Ibid*, p. 306.

Proper 12, Year A
Pentecost 10
Ordinary Time 17
Romans 8:26-39

Confidence In Prayer

*Likewise the Spirit helps us in our weakness; for we do
not know how to pray as we ought, but that very Spirit
intercedes with sighs too deep for words. And God, who
searches the heart, knows what is the mind of the Spirit,
because the Spirit intercedes for the saints according
to the will of God.... Who will separate us from the love
of Christ? Will hardship, or distress, or persecution, or
famine, or nakedness, or peril, or sword? As it is written, "For your sake we are being killed all day long;
we are accounted as sheep to be slaughtered." No, in
all these things we are more than conquerors through
him who loved us. For I am convinced that neither
death, nor life, nor angels, nor rulers, nor things present,
nor things to come, nor powers, nor height, nor depth,
nor anything else in all creation, will be able to separate us from the love of God in Christ Jesus our Lord.*
— Romans 8:26-27, 35-39

My subject this morning is prayer, taking as inspiration the
reassuring words of Saint Paul: "The Spirit helps us in our weakness, for we do not know how to pray as we ought, but that very
Spirit intercedes for us with sighs too deep for words."

The Spirit helps us. I believe that God wants us to have confidence in prayer, confidence to approach God freely and frequently
with the concerns of our hearts. But it's hard to feel that kind of
confidence when, like Saint Paul, we don't know how to pray and
aren't sure what to expect when we do. There's good reason for us
to be uncertain or ambivalent about prayer — intellectually, we
want to know how prayer "works" in a way that makes sense, while

our hearers are afraid to be disappointed or duped. We want to open, but not naive; faithful, yet not misguided in prayer.

I read an article about Joel Osteen, the head pastor of Lakewood Community Church in Houston, Texas, which draws 30,000 people each week for worship. This is the church that purchased the former stadium of the Houston Rockets for its worship site. Lakewood is clearly doing some things right. The congregation is racially and socio-economically integrated in ways that a church like ours can't even imagine. And Osteen's message of God's love speaks to whole segments of our population that liberal Christianity has written off for years.

Osteen has a fascinating view of prayer — one that encourages us to believe that God wants only good things for us, defined mostly in terms of material wealth, physical attractiveness, and happy relationships. We needn't be satisfied with mediocre lives, he says. "You have to start believing that good things are coming your way, and they will!" He's not completely off the mark, as far as I can tell. There is some gospel in what he says, and people are genuinely drawn to him. There is also sufficient distortion and superficiality in his teachings that others, looking to him as an example of Christian leadership, could rightfully discard the entire Christian enterprise as a rationalization for American self-preoccupation and greed. Still others, like those of us who want to follow Jesus and yet are acutely aware of how prayer can serve to reinforce our own biases and wishful thinking, might be left somewhat paralyzed, unsure how to articulate what we think or believe about prayer.[1]

The scriptures have much to teach us here. There's a story in the gospel of Luke in which Jesus has just finished a time apart from his disciples — his prayer time with God — and they ask him to teach them how to pray. He says to them, "When you pray say: Father, hallowed be your name. Your kingdom come. Give us each day our daily bread. And forgive us our sins, for we ourselves forgive everyone indebted to us. And do not bring us to the time of trial" (Luke 11:1-4). These are straightforward words of request, for sufficient food and forgiveness and to be spared from hardship. A recent biblical paraphrase interprets the Lord's Prayer this way:

"Father, reveal who you are. Set the world right. Keep us alive with three square meals. Keep us forgiven with you and forgiving others. Keep us safe from ourselves and from evil."[2]

After teaching his disciples words to pray, Jesus tells them two stories: the first is of a man going to his friend's house in the middle of the night asking for bread and the friend answering the door because of the man's persistence; the second is of parents whose child asks for a fish to eat. "Is there anyone among you," Jesus asks, "who, if your child asks for a fish will give a snake instead?" Jesus wants us to trust in God's love and to persevere in prayer: "Ask," he says, "and it will be given you; search, and you will find" (Luke 11:9).

This is the simple, foundational prayer, of bringing our concerns and needs before God. It requires no expertise, liturgical structure, or intermediaries. It doesn't depend on a particular view of who or what God is; it asks only that we acknowledge that mysterious presence at the center of all things to which Jesus himself entrusted his life. Praying in this way does require honesty, however, with ourselves and with God. In the words of theologian, Marjorie Suchocki, "Prayer is not the place for pretend piety; prayer is the place for getting down to brass tacks. Emotions that one might hesitate to express in conversation with others are appropriately expressed in prayer ... God receives us as we are, and who we are is no surprise to God."[3]

But does this mean that prayer is simply a matter of asking for what we want? Are those who preach the prosperity gospel so prevalent in this country right? Jesus' words seem to imply — ask and it will be given you. Yet there is more to prayer than asking; Jesus himself knew that. "Father, if it be possible, let this cup pass from me," he prayed in the Garden of Gethsemane. "But your will, not mine, be done." In addition to honestly placing our desires before God, there is something in prayer that has to do with acceptance and surrender to all that is beyond our control.

The Jesuit storyteller, Anthony de Mello, wrote of a spiritual leader whose disciples wanted him to teach them how to pray. He responded this way:

*Two men were once walking through a field when they
saw an angry bull. Instantly they made for the nearest
fence with the bull in hot pursuit. It soon became evi-
dent to them that they weren't going to make it, so one
man shouted to another, "We've had it! Nothing can
save us. Say a prayer. Quick!" The other shouted back,
"I've never prayed in my life and I don't exactly have a
prayer for this occasion." "Never mind," the other
yelled back. "The bull is catching up with us. Any prayer
will do." So he said the one he remembered his father
used to say before meals, "For what we are about to
receive, Lord, make us truly grateful."*[4]

Nothing, de Mello concludes, surpasses the holiness of those
who have learned to accept everything that is. "In the game of
cards called life," he writes, "one plays the hand one is dealt to the
best of one's ability."[5] Which, if you think about it, is another way
of saying, "Not my will, but yours be done." Saint Paul writes of a
similar moment of surrender and acceptance in his life, in reference to something he refers to as "a thorn in his flesh." We don't
know what the thorn was; as you can imagine, there is all sorts of
speculation about it. Whatever it was, Paul asked in prayer that it
be removed. "Three times I appealed to the Lord about this, that it
would leave me, but he said to me, 'My grace is sufficient for you,
for power is made perfect in weakness' " (2 Corinthians 12:9).

Then there is the kind of prayer that asks for change, not in the
circumstances around us, but in our response to them. It's prayer
that takes us beyond acceptance, I think, to personal transformation. Again, in the words of Marjorie Suchocki, "We pray to God
from where we are, not where we consider we should be. And God,
who knows us where we are, can lead us to where we can be."[6]
"Change not one thing in my life," I once heard a very courageous
person pray, "instead, change me." Change me. Take my heart of
stone and give me a heart of flesh. Take my selfish, frightened soul
and make of me a person of generosity and love. Allow me to live
with joy in a broken, troubled world. To echo the words of St.
Francis of Assisi, "Where there is hatred, let me sow love." My

spiritual director said to me recently, "Resilience is the transformation of grief into compassion."

This may be the hardest prayer of all, and yet the most freeing. It shifts our perspective, ever so slowly, away from what we want and how we imagine other people or circumstances must change in order for us to be happy, toward God and God's capacity to change our hearts. It opens up the possibility of cooperation with God in the redeeming of the world. Suchocki writes, "What if prayer increases the effectiveness of God's presence in the world? God works in the world as it is in order to bring it to where it can be. When we pray, we open ourselves to be part of that creative, loving work of God."[7]

My favorite description of prayer comes from the novel by Louise Erdrich titled *The Last Report on the Miracles at Little No Horse*. It tells the story of a woman named Agnes who lives most of her life disguised as a male priest, Father Damien, living among the Ojibwe people in Northern Minnesota. Hers is a long and complex story, as you can imagine, but she loves being a priest. She loves being Father Damien. Yet, the cost of her life is high. How does she cope?

"Four times a day," Erdich wrote, "on rising, at noon, late afternoon, and before going to bed, Agnes and Father Damien become one person who addresses the unknown. The priest stops what he is doing, makes himself transparent, and breaks himself open. That is, he prays." He prays that the warring factions among his people will dissolve their hatred. He prays for the conversion of one of the native leaders and then prays for his own enlightenment in case converting another is a mistake. Agnes prays for a cheerful spirit and for her dangerous longings to cease. And she prays to better understand the Ojibwe language and its mysterious effect on the experience of God. She begins to address the trinity as four, to include the spirit of each direction — those who sit at the four corners of the earth. There, at the center, she allows herself to fall apart. "What a relief it was, in those moments, to be nothing, and to have no thought or expectations." Then she rises, rubs her eyes, and goes on in Father Damien's skin. She quietly and unassumingly goes back to work, back to her life and her service, as faithfully as she can.[8]

I offer you these images of prayer: first, as honest, personal communication, laying before God the concerns and desires of our hearts; second, as acceptance, learning, by grace, to surrender to the things that cannot be changed; and finally, as transformation, allowing ourselves to be changed, by life and by prayer, into compassionate, generous people, partners with God in the loving and reshaping of the world. The most important words to remember are those with which we started, from Saint Paul's letter to the Romans, which assures us that no matter how ambivalent, uncertain, unbelieving, uninformed, and inexperienced we may be in prayer, the Spirit of God that dwells within us helps us to pray, beyond language, with sighs too deep for words. And there is nothing, Saint Paul says, nothing at all, that can ever separate us from the love of God in Christ Jesus.

1. Jason Byasse, "Be Happy: The Health and Wealth Gospel," in *The Christian Century*, July 12, 2005, pp. 20-22.

2. Eugene Peterson, *The Message: The New Testament in Contemporary Language, Like You've Never Read It Before* (Colorado Springs: NavPress, 1994), p. 146.

3. Marjorie Suchocki, *In God's Presence: Theological Reflections on Prayer* (St. Louis: Chalice Press, 1996), pp. 37-38.

4. Anthony de Mello, S.J., *Taking Flight: A Book of Story Meditations* (New York: Doubleday, 1988), p. 31.

5. *Ibid.*

6. *Op cit*, Suchocki, p. 38.

7. *Op cit*, Suchocki, p. 18.

8. Louise Erdrich, *The Last Report on the Miracles at Little No Horse* (New York: HarperCollins, 2001), p. 182.

Proper 16, Year A
Pentecost 14
Ordinary Time 21
Matthew 16:13-20

How Well Do You Know Him?

> *Now when Jesus came into the district of Caesarea*
> *Philippi, he asked his disciples, "Who do people say*
> *that the Son of Man is?" And they said, "Some say John*
> *the Baptist, but others Elijah, and still others Jeremiah*
> *or one of the prophets." He said to them, "But who do*
> *you say that I am?" Simon Peter answered, "You are*
> *the Messiah, the Son of the living God." And Jesus an-*
> *swered, "Blessed are you, Simon son of Jonah! For flesh*
> *and blood has not revealed this to you, but my Father*
> *in heaven. And I tell you, you are Peter, and on this*
> *rock I will build my church, and the gates of Hades will*
> *not prevail against it. I will give you the keys of the*
> *kingdom of heaven, and whatever you bind on earth*
> *will be bound in heaven, and whatever you loose on*
> *earth will be loosed in heaven." Then he sternly or-*
> *dered the disciples not to tell anyone that he was the*
> *Messiah.*   — Matthew 16:13-20

It's a rule in family systems theory that whatever you or I might say about another person reveals more about us than the person we're describing. Everything about us, in other words, colors our perceptions of another. Thus when we consider how we might answer Jesus' question, "Who do you say that I am?" we need to start with ourselves, who we are, and all that influences how we speak of anyone, including Jesus.

From the world of children's literature comes this classic exchange on the question of identity:

> *"Who are you?" said the Caterpillar. This was not an*
> *encouraging opening for a conversation. Alice replied,*

*rather shyly, "I hardly know, sir, just at present — at
least I know who I was when I got up this morning, but
I think I must have been changed several times since
then. "What do you mean by that?" said the Caterpil-
lar sternly, "Explain yourself!" "I can't explain myself, I'm afraid, sir," said Alice, "Because I'm not myself, you see."*[1]

Our experience of Jesus is connected to how we experience being
ourselves. There's no judgment in that. It's simply the place to begin when attempting to answer that bedrock question of Christian
faith: "Who do we say that Jesus is?"

From that place of self-awareness, we turn our gaze toward
him. How well do we know Jesus? The honest answer for many,
and surely for most of us at least some of the time, is, not very
well. We may think we know, but do we, really? How much have
we assimilated, and perhaps rejected, the caricatures of Jesus so
prevalent in our culture? How much time have we spent getting to
know him? And if we wanted to get to know him better, where
would we begin?

The best place to learn about Jesus, in my opinion, is in the
Bible. Pick up a Bible — make sure that it's a decent translation —
find the beginning of the New Testament and read. The first four
books, the gospels of Matthew, Mark, Luke, and John, are neither
long nor difficult. You could read one a week and be finished without taking anymore time than you spend reading the newspaper,
checking your email, or watching television. Even if you have read
the gospels many times before, and rightfully considered yourself
knowledgeable of their content, if you started today and read them
through again, you would learn something new about Jesus this
time around, and about yourself, simply by taking note of what
catches your attention.

Don't expect to understand or agree with everything you read
about him, because you won't. Don't expect the accounts to be
consistent, lacking in contradictions, because they aren't. Don't
expect to be comforted or challenged by all that you read, though
you will at times be both comforted and challenged to the core.

Don't expect that Jesus will agree with all of your politics; if he does, you aren't reading deeply enough. Expect to be offended sometimes, and at other times moved to the point of tears. Most important, expect on occasion to be *spoken to*, as if the words were written for you. Approach the gospels with an open mind and discerning heart. Bring all of your doubts and questions, but as the protagonist of the novel, *Gilead*, writes in a letter to his son, "Make sure that the doubts and questions are your own, not, so to speak, the mustache and walking stick that happen to be the fashion of any particular moment."[2]

A few years ago, I heard a radio interview with the musician, Bobby McFerrin, when he was in the Twin Cities to perform in a choral music festival. McFerrin, as you may know, is a devout Christian. His faith in Jesus is his guiding light. One of his practices is to pray and meditate daily and always for half an hour prior to every stage performance. In fact, his plane was delayed on the day of his performance here, and he arrived at the concert hall just at the time he was to go on stage. But so important is his discipline of prayer, that he delayed the show for half an hour. The radio interviewer asked McFerrin how he spent that time. "These days," he said, "I'm reading the gospels of Jesus. There are so many terrible things being done in the name of religion now, including Christianity. I want to get closer to Jesus. I want to know what he said and did, not what others say about him or do in his name."

I came across a similar account of steady Bible reading recently, although I wouldn't have guessed it from the essay's opening sentence. The author began: "When I was in Croatia this past May, I went on a hunt for sausage. Not any kind of sausage mind you, but for *kulen*, a specialty from a region in northeast Croatia. You can't buy it in any store. To get it you've got to have friends in high places — in backwater villages of Slavonia where people raise their own pigs and prepare *kulen* according to recipes passed on in families for generations."

A former student had such a friend and together they drove off into the remote countryside. Their destination: "... one of those nondescript houses on a nondescript village street with ditches dug along the road as a sewer system. There was no TV antenna, let alone a satellite dish — otherwise ubiquitous in many Croatian towns. As we entered the kitchen, which also functioned as a living room, I saw on the table an open Bible. Our host was obviously reading it when we came in and it was a Bible well-worn from use."

As they sat around the table, shared *kulen* and wine, they embarked on a conversation about the Christian life. The author marveled at the depth of it. They weren't just exchanging pleasantries about the weather or sports or even complaining about politics and an inefficient economy. "If the Bible is the book you read," he wrote, "your conversations will likely concern the deep questions of life rather than skirt them. Compared with the way most of us spend our evenings in the West, the true marvel was that here was a man of one book. Instead of sinking down in front of a television or going to a village pub to drink down the hardship of his dreary existence, evening after evening he read the Bible and meditated on it."[3] Through his daily reading this Croatian farmer no doubt has a solid understanding of who Jesus is, one not easily shaken by the distortions that pass as Christian teachings in so much of our world.

I suggest that we commit to a similar discipline of regular Bible reading, so that we might know Jesus better and know ourselves at the depth to which he calls us. There is so much that conspires to keep us focused on things that don't matter. There is too much that passes for Christianity that simply mirrors the unrelenting self-absorption and naiveté of our culture. There are so many imposters who highjack the sincere religious sentiments of others for their own purposes.

Several members of the congregation have sent me an article circulating the internet titled, "The Christian Paradox: How a Faithful Nation Gets Jesus Wrong." The author, Bill McKibben, himself a Christian, begins by citing the statistics of Christian self-identification in America — among the highest in the world — and then the statistics of biblical illiteracy: "Only 40% of Americans can name more than four of the Ten Commandments. Less than 50% can cite any of the four authors of the gospels. Twelve percent believe Joan of Arc was Noah's wife."[4]

None of this, while embarrassing, is important, McKibben writes, in spiritual and political terms. Here is one statistic that does matter: "Three quarters of Americans believe the Bible teaches that 'God helps those who help themselves.' That is, three out four Americans believe this notion, which is at the core of our current individualist politics and culture, and was in fact uttered by Ben Franklin, actually appears in Scripture."[5] And while there are certainly examples in scripture of God helping the self-motivated, as McKibben points out, few ideas could be further from the Jesus' core teachings to love one's neighbor. On this essential matter, most American Christians are simply wrong. On this essential matter, most American Christians do not know Jesus and what he stands for, and yet they are convinced otherwise.

We need to know Jesus well enough to counter such anti-Christian Christianity with his message of sacrificial love. We need to know Jesus well enough to counter the voices in our heads that would have us doubt that the love we are to share is meant for us, too. We need to know Jesus well enough to trust that God's love is real; that God's forgiveness is real; that the strength and courage and guidance available to us in Christ is real; and that the call to walk the narrow path of discipleship is worth the sacrifice required.

Who do you say that Jesus is? From what basis of self-awareness and knowledge of him do you speak? Would you like to know him better?

There is another path to knowing him, that of mystical experience, which is available to us more than we realize. In the book, *Gilead*, a dying father writes to his young son, communicating all that he wishes he could tell him in person when the boy is older. He writes of one of the most important experiences of his life: a time when he and his father went to help take down the remains of a church that had burned.

> *Lightning had struck the steeple and the steeple fell into the building. It was raining the day we went to take the church down. All kinds of people came to help. The men who were working in the ruins got entirely black and filthy, till you would hardly know one from*

175

another. At the day's end, my father brought me some biscuit that had soot on it from his hands. I remember my father down on his heels in the rain, water dripping from his hat, feeding me biscuit from his scorched hand, with that old blackened wreck of a church behind him and steam rising where the rain fell on embers, the rain falling in gusts and the women singing "The Old Rugged Cross" while they saw to things, moving so gently as if they were dancing to the hymn. It was so joyful and sad. It seems to me that much of my life was comprehended in that moment. Grief itself has often returned to me that morning, when I took communion from my father's hand. I remember it as communion, and I believe that's what it was.[6]

"If only I could give you what my father gave me," he wrote to his son and then corrected himself. "No, what the Lord has given me and must also give you. But I hope you will put yourself in the way of the gift."

We cannot force or fake the gift of Jesus' presence in our life. But we can put ourselves in the way of the gift, by putting ourselves in the places that matter, stepping away from our screens of choice and reading our sacred texts, tending to our relationships and to our world, and seeking out those who can guide us to a deeper place. The presence of Jesus is a gift that changes us, as surely as her many adventures changed Alice. And it changes forever how we answer the question Jesus asked his disciples so long ago: Who do you say that I am?

---

1. Lewis Carroll, *Alice's Adventures in Wonderland* (London: William Heinemann, Ltd, 1862), p. 49.

2. Marilynne Robinson, *Gilead* (New York: Farrar, Straus, & Giroux, 2004), p. 179.

3. Miroslav Volf, "Not by Sausage Alone," in *The Christian Century*, August 9, 2005, p. 32.

4. Bill McKibben, "The Christian Paradox: How a Faithful Nation Gets Jesus Wrong," in *Harpers* magazine, August 2005, pp. 2-3.

5. *Ibid.*

6. *Op cit*, Robinson, p. 114.

Proper 18, Year C
Pentecost 16
Ordinary Time 23 or
Labor Day
Jeremiah 18:1-11
Luke 14:25-33

Work And Rest

The word that came to Jeremiah from the Lord: "Come, go down to the potter's house, and there I will let you hear my words." So I went down to the potter's house, and here he was working at his wheel.
— Jeremiah 18:1-3

Now large crowds were traveling with him; and he turned and said to them: "Whoever comes to me and does not hate father and mother, wife and children, brothers and sisters, yes, and even life itself, cannot be my disciple. Whoever does not carry the cross and follow me cannot be my disciple. For which of you, intending to build a tower, does not first sit down and estimate the cost, to see whether he has enough to complete it? Otherwise, when he has laid a foundation and is not able to finish, all who see it will begin to ridicule him, saying, 'This fellow began to build and was not able to finish.' Or what king, going out to wage war against another king, will not sit down first and consider whether he is able with ten thousand to oppose the one who comes against him with twenty thousand? If he cannot, then, while the other is still far away, he sends a delegation and asks for the terms of peace. So therefore, none of you can become my disciple if you do not give up all your possessions."
— Luke 14:25-33

The observance of Labor Day began in the late 1800s, both as a celebration and protest, as workers took an unpaid day off to gather in New York City's Union Square. The idea of a holiday devoted to Labor's cause spread across various states and was eventually shepherded through the US Congress, mostly in an effort to calm the intense labor tensions of the time. President Grover Cleveland, running for reelection, signed the legislation six days after he sent 12,000 federal troops to break a railroad workers' strike in Pullman, Illinois.

As a reelection strategy, it didn't work; Cleveland lost. However, Labor Day remains, no longer a protest and not so much a celebration of labor as a break from it. It's fitting that we honor those upon whose labors our lives depend by giving them a day off. It's good to honor our own work by stepping away from it for a day. And it's very nice to be able to catch our breath as summer gives way to fall and as life, for many, steps up to a decidedly busier pace.

One of the best things about the summer we're saying goodbye to was the opportunities it gave to take a break from whatever we consider normal routines and rediscover, for either short or long periods of time, a more relaxed way of living. My long stretch of rest came earlier in the year, during the gift of sabbatical from February to May. As a result, like many of you I worked through the summer, with a few shorter breaks — a day, a weekend, four glorious days in northern Minnesota.

Throughout the summer, precisely because I was working, I tried to practice the art of sabbath. How could I learn to stop working at the end of day, not because I had finished my work, but because the time of work had ended? How could I let go of the problems that nagged at my consciousness and allow myself the luxury of reading a novel or relaxing with family? What would life be like if I allowed myself, at last, to get enough sleep?

The Jewish writer, Abraham Joshua Heschel, writes of sabbath in this way:

> *The sabbath as a day of rest, as a day of abstaining from toil, is not for the purpose of recovering one's lost strength and becoming fit for the forthcoming labor.*

*The sabbath is a day for the sake of life. We are not
beasts of burden and the sabbath is not for the purpose
of increasing the efficiency of our work. It is not an
interlude, but the climax of living.*[1]

He goes on:

*It must always be remembered that the sabbath is not
an occasion for diversion or frivolity; not a day to shoot
fireworks or to turn somersaults, but an opportunity to
mend our tattered lives.*[2]

Mending our tattered lives. How we need that. It's a standard,
almost cliché, critique of modern society that in our busyness we
have lost the essential rhythm between work and rest. The philoso-
pher, Jacob Needleman, calls it a new kind of poverty and the effects of it are everywhere. "Because we do not rest," writes the
author Wayne Muller, "we lose our way. We miss the compass points
that show us where to go. We bypass the nourishment that would
give us succor. We miss the quiet that would give us wisdom. For
want of rest, our lives are in danger."[3]

There are many ways that the lack of sabbath costs us, all that
we lose when we miss the gift of living, being present, taking time
for nourishment and renewal. On this Labor Day weekend, I'd like
to focus, with due respect to Heschel, on the cost to our *work* when
we don't step away from it regularly, how our work is compromised when we lose sight of the need to rest and mend the tattered
places in us. In speaking of work, I don't mean simply what some
of us do for a paycheck, but all aspects of life's labors. The union
organizer, Si Kahn, wrote in a song, "Your life is more than your
work. And your work is more than your job." What happens to our
life and our work when we don't take adequate time away?

A friend of mine spent the last two years of her father's life
monitoring his care from four states away. As a nurse, she had the
expertise her family relied on to navigate the maze of health care
and hospitalization. Every other week she would drive or take the
train to her parents' home to care for them, meet with doctors, or
make new arrangements for his treatment. In the meantime she

tried to keep up with her own life — her work, children, friends, and community ties. All in all, she said, she managed pretty well, or so she thought until the nurse taking her father's blood pressure offered to check hers, too. She was normally a very healthy person and while she seemed fine to everyone, including herself, her blood pressure had risen to dangerous levels and she had no awareness of it. What gave her pause wasn't so much concern for her own health, but rather the realization that she was making life and death decisions on her father's behalf in such a compromised state, all the more dangerous because she thought she was fine.

It's almost impossible to make good decisions under pressure, when we don't have the time to consider the consequences of our choices. One of the downsides of electronic communication, it seems to me, is that we have set ourselves the standard of instant response. No longer is there time for measured reflection, a chance to think before reacting. We expect answers right away.

I get nervous every legislative session watching the frenetic pace of public officials and those who work for them. It's as if sleep deprivation is a requirement of public office. And what does all the frenetic energy produce? To make his own point about being prepared and ready for work, Jesus gave the example of a king discerning whether or not to go to war. Whatever your views of the current war in Iraq, no one disputes the fact that in our country's rush to go to war we made grave miscalculations of its cost. Our understanding of what we, in fact, were there to fight and how we would be perceived was woefully inaccurate. No matter how noble our efforts and how sincere the soldiers were that we sent to fight, because we sent them under mistaken premises and ill-prepared for the reality awaiting them, our good intentions have had, in many instances, made things worse rather than better for the Iraqi people. We may have created, rather than destroyed, the ideal environment for terrorism.

This dangerous action without reflection is not unique to politics. As Wayne Muller wrote, even among those dedicated to the service of others, "the corrosive pressure of frantic overactivity can cause suffering in ourselves and others ... With few notable exceptions, the way we solve problems in all fields of public service is reactively, quickly, and badly. It's naive to assume that our good intentions protect us from doing unintended harm. Doing good requires more than hard work. We need time to step back, reflect on past actions, and be quiet enough to recognize what is good."[4]

Scripture speaks often and well about the spiritual implications of our work and of the need for rest from it. The Bible begins, you recall, with a creation story in which God created the heavens, the earth, and every living thing, including humankind in God's own likeness, and then rested on the seventh day. Like God, our lives are best lived in such a rhythm of work and rest. In the passage read this morning from the prophet Jeremiah, he likens God's creative work to that of a potter at his wheel, able to craft, mold, and even destroy clay at his will. Jeremiah's point is that God is like the potter, but it's also true that we, as potters, are like God — able to craft, mold, and even destroy. Our creative work is our most godlike potential, an awesome gift and responsibility.

Jesus speaks to us rather harshly this morning about the importance of being prepared and willing to sacrifice if we want to take up the work of following him. No more gentle talk about his yoke being easy and his burden light. This will be hard, he says, like carrying a cross. It will require preparation and foresight, careful discernment and persistent effort. Think it through carefully — are you up for it?

Keep in mind that he speaks this way as he has realized the cost of his vocation for himself. After three years of ministry in Galilee, healing the sick, teaching in synagogues, forming his disciples; three years of frequent time away to pray, reflect, and consider his life's purpose, now he knows what he is to do and where he is to accomplish it. He's on his way to Jerusalem, now like all the great prophets before him. He's going back to his Father's house, the temple where he had sat as a twelve-year-old boy listening to the wisdom of his elders. He would confront the religious hypocrisy and abuse of temple leadership and give his life in witness to truth. I don't think he meant to be harsh as he told his disciples to measure the cost of following him. He was simply clear and wanted them to know that he could not spare them the cost he himself was willing to pay.

Every once in a while life asks of us that kind of clarity, that kind of conviction and total commitment. It doesn't happen all the time, thank goodness, but pity the person for whom it never happens, for it is a sign of a life truly lived. William Sloan Coffin once wrote, "It is not so much the unexamined life that is not worth living, but the uncommitted one." And yet how are we to know when such commitment and focused effort is required? How can we discern a true calling from a false one, a cause worthy of our lives from one that will simply deplete it, the things that are worth dying for from the things that aren't? When our true work invites us to give our life to it, how will we recognize it for what it is?

One very simple and life-giving way is to establish a rhythm of rest and reflection that allows us to ponder the deeper meaning of things, to renew our minds and spirits with the joys of living. For we will never be free to say yes to the great things life asks of us if we are so exhausted from the little things that we can't see the forest from the trees. We're learning that before we can discern our greatest calling as a community we have to let go of some things that drain our energy and creative spirit. If we are to find our path, wherever it will lead, we simply must make regular time and space for rest, relaxation, and prayer — not only in the seasons that allow it, like the summer that is ending, but also, and especially, in the busy ones that work against it, like the one before us. In that quiet, restful space will come the clarity and conviction to follow Jesus where he leads and fully engage the work that is ours.

---

1. Abraham Joshua Heschel, *The Sabbath* (New York: HarperCollins, 1951), p. 14.

2. *Ibid*, p. 18.

3. Wayne Muller, *Sabbath: Restoring the Sacred Rhythm of Rest* (Bantam Books, 1991), p. 1.

4. *Ibid*, p. 163.

Nothing, Some, Or All

The Pharisees went and plotted to entrap him in what he said. So they sent their disciples to him, along with the Herodians, saying, "Teacher, we know that you are sincere, and teach the way of God in accordance with truth, and show deference to no one; for you do not regard people with partiality. Tell us, then, what you think. Is it lawful to pay taxes to the emperor, or not?" But Jesus, aware of their malice, said, "Why are you putting me to the test, you hypocrites? Show me the coin used for the tax." And they brought him a denarius. Then he said to them, "Whose head is this, and whose title?" They answered, "The emperor's." Then he said to them, "Give therefore to the emperor the things that are the emperor's and to God the things that are God's." When they heard this, they were amazed; and they left him and went away. — Matthew 22:15-22

I'd like to begin with a series of quotes, and then a story.

The first comes from the novel, *Four Souls*, by Louise Erdrich, and is a meditation on time:

Time is the water in which we live, and we breathe it like fish. It's hard to swim against the current. Time is an element no human has mastered; we are all bound to go where we are sent. There is only time. For what are we all but bits of time caught for a moment in a tangle of blood, bones, skin, and brain? We are time's containers. Time pours into us and then pours out again. In between the two pourings, we live our destiny.[1]

185

The second is a word of wisdom from the monk/writer Thomas Merton on the difference between pleasure and joy:

> *Do not look for any rest in pleasure, because you were not created for pleasure: you were created for joy. And if you do not know the difference between pleasure and joy, you have not begun to live.*[2]

The third is from the opening chapter of Rick Warren's book, *The Purpose-Driven Life*:

> *It's not about you. The purpose of your life is far greater than your own personal fulfillment, your peace of mind, or even your happiness. It's far greater than your family, your career, or even your wildest dreams and ambitions. If you want to know why you were placed on this planet, you must begin with God.*[3]

Those are the quotes: In between time pouring in and out of us, we live our destiny; we were created not for pleasure, but for joy; the purpose of our lives rests in God. Now the story:

> *There once was a man who collected fine pearls. Pearls were both his passion and his profession, as he searched the world over for the finest pearls and made his fortune selling them to others. One day he heard of an exquisite pearl for sale in a pawn shop on the other side of town and he jumped in his car to investigate. Sure enough, beneath the dust and debris of a dilapidated store, he found the pearl, more beautiful than any he had ever seen or been privileged to own. "What do you want for this pearl?" he asked the shop owner. "Oh, I don't know," the owner replied. "What do you got?" The man opened his wallet: "I have $223," he said. "All right, I'll take it," the owner said. "What else do you got?" "I have a credit card with a $1,000 spending limit," he said. "Okay, I'll take that, too. What else?" As if bewitched by this pearl, the man began to barter everything he owned: his car, his house. In his*

delusion he thought he could give away his wife and two kids. And the shopkeeper kept on saying, "Okay. I'll take that. What else you got?" Until there was nothing left.

The man took the pearl and was about to leave. The shopkeeper stopped him and said, "You know the last thing I need is another wife and two kids. You take yours back. But remember, they don't belong to you. And I don't need another house. You take yours. But remember, it doesn't belong to you." And so it went — the shop owner gave him everything back — his car, his credit card, even the $223 in his wallet. "But remember: your life doesn't belong to you."[4]

When Jesus said, in response to the Pharisees' baiting him on the question of taxes, "Give to the emperor the things that are the emperor's and to God the things that are God's," he wasn't being flip. He meant it: Give the world its due; but give to God the things that are God's. But he left us to answer the question for ourselves: What belongs to God?

I can think of three possible answers: The first: *nothing.* Nothing of who we are, have been given, or have earned belongs to God. The second: *Some portion* of who we are, what we have been given, or have earned belongs to God. Or, the third: *everything.* Everything we are, have been given, or have earned belongs not to us, but to God.

We hear the first answer loud and clear in the predominant voices of our culture. God. Instead of Rick Warren's assertion: "It's not about you," our culture cries out, "It's *all* about you. You take it all; you need it all; you deserve it all." Not only is it all about us, it's all *up* to us, too. We're essentially on our own. Our destiny is ours to figure out or to give away to the most urgent pressure, nagging anxiety, or tantalizing pleasure that overtakes us.

Fortunately, "Nothing belongs to God" isn't an answer that satisfies for long. For those of us who feel or hunger for the presence of God in our lives, it rings hollow even as we find ourselves periodically seduced by it. Somehow we know that we were not created for nothing, that there is a greater purpose to life than consumption, a larger canvas on which to work than simply the backdrop of what we can figure out or make happen on our own. We have this need, this desire to give, and not only to give but to give *back* something of all that is entrusted to us.

That would lead us to consider the second answer to the question, "What belongs to God?" *Some portion* of who we are, what we've been given, or have earned belongs to God. *Some portion* — there's significant spiritual energy around this idea of giving back some portion of our lives to God. In scripture there are the ancient stories of the Israelites giving the firstfruits of their harvest to the temple and the spiritual practice of not reaping to the very edges of their fields, so that there was always some left over for those not fortunate enough to own a field. There is the idea of a tithe: giving 10% of one's earnings, one's time, one's creative energies away to the glory of God and in service to others.

It's a good start to think in these terms. We all have to start somewhere in learning how to give in a world that overwhelmingly encourages us to take. We have to start somewhere in making conscious choices of generosity and commitment, rather than relying on our impulses to dictate where we invest ourselves. We all have to start somewhere in determining how we're going to make room for God — or practicing the awareness of God — in a society that values busyness above all. Thinking in proportional terms is a good start. Some of the time, some of the talent, some of the riches that seemingly belongs to us, in fact, belongs to God.

Once set aside, we have to decide *where* to give that proportion that belongs to God. But that's a secondary matter and far less important than the first. The first is to say: I will decide in advance of other pressures that some portion of my life belongs to God — be it Sunday morning in church, Thursday afternoons in ministry at a hospital or homeless shelter, the painstaking work of justice, the first ten minutes of the day or my final thoughts before falling asleep, or the time in my car when I would normally listen to the radio. Likewise, some portion of the talent I have been given belongs to God and some portion of my wealth belongs to God, and I will spend it accordingly.

The problem with this proportional way of thinking is that it can lead to compartmentalization in our understanding of spirituality, as if the part of us that goes to church on some Sunday mornings is our spiritual side — the part of us God cares about — and what we do at every other time isn't spiritual and isn't God's concern. It's as if the money we give to the church or to another charity is the money God has some authority over, and the rest is ours to spend as we like. It's as if our prayer time is enough to compensate for whatever we do when we're not, in fact, praying.

I'm sensitive to dangers of compartmentalizing faith, keeping God in a box of manageable commitments and reasonable expectations, in part because I'm often guilty of it. It is the sin of religious people. Proportional giving is a step up from living as if nothing belongs to God, and we're very proud of that fact, but frankly, it can lead to some of the worst forms of hypocrisy, the kind Jesus railed against when he saw it in the religious leaders of his day.

It's not true that God only cares about the side of our lives we choose to lift up or dedicate as religious. It's never been true. If the biblical prophets are right, God cares more about what we do Monday through Saturday than whether or not we show up in church on Sunday mornings. If the prophets are right, God cares more about how we spend the money we keep than the money we give away. If the prophets are right, God cares about everything, this God to whom our hearts are open, all desires known, and from whom no secrets are hid. In God's eyes we aren't divided up into neat categories, one of which, for those of us who choose it, is religious. God cares about and has a claim on it all.

Here's the thing. While everything about us belongs to God, what does God do? Like the shopkeeper, God gives it all back. God gives everything back to us and in essence, says, "I love you. I created you for joy and meaning and your own unique destiny. Go and spend yourself lavishly and freely; claim your life and make of it what you will in the joys and tribulations of living. I'm here to help, but only if you ask. I'm here to receive, but only what you choose to give."

189

One of my first teachers of generosity taught me to set aside 10% of what I earn for the work of God in the world. He said, "Much good will come from your giving, and you will have the satisfaction of learning generosity. But what matters most to God is how the 10% you give informs the 90% you keep."

A long time ago, I decided to give a proportion of my life away; I need to be reminded daily that everything I have belongs to God. Starting with some portion helps. It's a practice I began long before I became a priest and it will carry me far beyond the days when the largest percentage of the 10% I give to God goes to the church.

We are in the season of stewardship, during which we ask you to consider your gifts, so let me say this: I am grateful to be your rector. I'm grateful to be part of a plucky, courageous, generous, risk-taking congregation, one that challenges me on a daily basis to grow in love. I am inspired by this parish's lay leadership, the many people who dedicate significant portions of their own life and hard-earned resources to the glory of God in this place, and who ensure that every dollar invested here is spent transparently, prudently, and at times lavishly for the gospel's sake. I am delighted to be in a place in my life that I am able to give to a capital campaign that will strengthen and enhance this congregation's ministry long after I am no longer your rector. I'm awed by those who call us to set our sights high and to have pledged far more than what is comfortable in faithfulness to a vision of what our church can be. I'm proud to take my place to be among them. I pray that you are equally grateful, inspired, and proud to give here. If not, then perhaps you shouldn't give, for God wants our gifts to be freely and joyfully given.

We have but a short time on this earth. We were not created for pleasure, but for joy. Our life's purpose is far bigger than we will ever know. Nothing we think we own really belongs to us. But God gives everything to us — for a time — to enjoy, to steward, to share, and to give back with gratitude. "Give therefore to the emperor the things that are the emperor's and to God the things that are God's."

1. Louise Erdrich, *Four Souls* (New York: Harper Perennial, 2004), p. 28.

2. Thomas Merton, source unknown. Quoted by Greg Rickel in "Joy or Pleasure? Stewardship as a Transformed Life."

3. Rick Warren, *The Purpose-Driven Life* (Grand Rapids, Michigan: Zondervan, 2002), p. 17.

4. As told by Greg Rickel in a workshop on stewardship in the Diocese of Minnesota, September 2005.

All Saints, Year A
Ecclesiasticus 44:1-10, 13-14
Matthew 5:1-12

Character Is A Lifetime Job

Some of them have left behind a name, so that others declare their praise. But of others there is no memory; they have perished as though they had never existed; they have become as though they had never been born, they and their children after them. But these also were godly men, whose righteous deeds have not been forgotten ... Their offspring will continue forever, and their glory will never be blotted out. Their bodies are buried in peace, but their name lives on generation after generation. — Ecclesiasticus 44:8-10, 13-14

When Jesus saw the crowds, he went up the mountain; and after he sat down, his disciples came to him. Then he began to speak, and taught them, saying, "Blessed are the poor in spirit, for theirs is the kingdom of heaven. Blessed are those who mourn, for they will be comforted. Blessed are the meek, for they will inherit the earth. Blessed are those who hunger and thirst for righteousness, for they will be filled. Blessed are the merciful, for they will receive mercy. Blessed are the pure in heart, for they will see God. Blessed are the peacemakers, for they will be called children of God. Blessed are those who are persecuted for righteousness' sake, for theirs is the kingdom of heaven. Blessed are you when people revile you and persecute you and utter all kinds of evil against you falsely on my account. Rejoice and be glad, for your reward is great in heaven, for in the same way they persecuted the prophets who were before you." — Matthew 5:1-12

In our dining room we have a set of silver candlesticks that belonged to my grandparents. When I light the candles, I think of

193

my grandmother. She loved eating by candlelight, even at breakfast, a love she passed on to my mother and to me. My grandmother was not a great person in the eyes of the world, or, at times, in the eyes of her family. She could be demanding, opinionated, and prickly. I have the distinct impression that it was harder to be one of her children than one of her grandchildren, and being her grandchild was no picnic. But I realize now, as I the light candles, how much I learned from her. She taught me the importance of paying attention to the small, daily tasks and responsibilities upon which a life is built. It was the way she carefully prepared each meal, set the table, and tended to her home. It was how she would rise each summer morning at 6 a.m. to lead an exercise class on the beach for her neighbors, and then go for a swim in the frigid North Sea before returning home to prepare breakfast. It was how she greeted us when we arrived for our visits with hot tea and princess torta (cake) — the staple of every Swedish celebration — and how she cried when we left, standing at the edge of the yard waving her handkerchief good-bye until we disappeared from view.

What I hear in the glorious themes of All Saints Sunday is a gentle call to persistence, faithfulness in the small things that help shape our character. Life isn't always easy or kind. While it can be exciting and even glamorous at times, it isn't that way very often and we best not get too attached to that kind of energy, or the rest of our life — which is to say, most of it — will seem dull by comparison. It may be that we'll be called upon once or twice in our lifetime for some extraordinary act of heroism or courage. But more likely our lives will be measured by small, steady acts of faithfulness and persistence. "The courage that counts is the courage of the every day," reads a note that someone once gave me. "Most of life involves putting one foot in front of the other. Big leaps have received too much press."

Big leaps have received too much press. The death of Rosa Parks brought back into public consciousness her big leap, when she decided not to give up her bus seat to a white person. "Rosa Parks was sick and tired of being sick and tired," the Secretary of State, Condoleezza Rice, said in her honor. It's a common, if misleading tribute to Rosa Parks' contribution to the Civil Rights

Movement, as if merely by sitting down she brought the South to its senses. History tells us otherwise. There were other African-American women arrested in that same year for refusing to give up their seat to a white person. Although NAACP lawyers were looking for a person to be the standard bearer for a legal challenge to the hated bus segregation laws, not one of them sparked a movement. But Rosa Parks did — less because of what she did and more because of the person she was.

She was a seamstress at a local department store *and* the secretary of the local NAACP chapter. She worked closely with all the rising African-American leaders of Montgomery who were aching for change. Twenty years ago, this is what the historian Taylor Branch wrote of Parks:

> *A tireless worker and churchgoer, of working-class station and middle-class demeanor, Rosa Parks was one of those rare people of whom everyone agreed that she gave more than she got. Her character represented one of the isolated blips on the graph of human nature, offsetting a dozen or more sociopaths. A Methodist herself, she served as teacher and mother figure to the kids of the NAACP Youth Council who met at a Lutheran Church near her home.*[1]

It is true that on December 1, 1955, she refused to give up her seat in what was known as "no man's land" — the open seats that either race could claim — when the driver demanded it. It is true that she was arrested. But that would have been the end of it were it not for the decision of the NAACP leadership to pursue a legal challenge on her behalf and a bus boycott organized by a new Baptist minister in town. That boycott, you recall, lasted over a year. Nothing would have happened if Parks herself, against the counsel of her family, had not agreed to be at the center of the storm: "If you think it will mean something to Montgomery and do some good," she said, "I'd be happy to go along with it." In other words, surrounding that one act of courage there were countless, largely invisible and forgotten acts of faithful persistence and the presence of a woman known above all for her unassuming, steadfast character. You don't build character in one dramatic moment. Building character is a lifetime job.

That's why so many stood for hours to pay their respects at her funeral, apart from the dignitaries there to bask secondhand in her light. The people came to her because she always came to them. She showed up in their churches and at their dedications; she taught in their schools and marched in their marches. She spent most of her ninety years working behind the scenes, in quiet, steady persistence.

Persistence is one of the most important, yet overlooked virtues. Why is persistence so important? Because life is not always easy or kind. God does not spare us from turmoil and struggle, and anyone who promises otherwise, in the words of Harvard chaplain Peter Gomes, "is either uninformed or lying and perhaps both, and owes no allegiance to the gospel." What God does in turmoil is strengthen us, giving us the capacity to keep going. "God is always by the side of those who need him," Gomes writes. "He is not in front to lead, not behind to push, not above to protect, but beside us to get us through."[2]

Or hear the gentle words of Archbishop Desmond Tutu, writing his latest book as if to each of us individually:

> *Dear Child of God, I am sorry to say that suffering is not optional. It seems to be part and parcel of the human condition, but suffering can either embitter or ennoble. Our suffering can become a spirituality of transformation when we understand that we have a role in God's work in the world. If we are to be true partners with God, we must learn to see with the eyes of God — that is, to see with the eyes of the heart. The eyes of the heart are not concerned with appearances but with essences, and as we cultivate these eyes we are able to learn from our suffering and to see the world with more loving, forgiving, and generous eyes.*[3]

Transformed suffering is the grace that enables us to persevere in love.

I believe this: Before Jesus sat down on the mountain to teach the crowd of people who had gathered to hear him, he first walked among them. He looked into the their faces and saw their struggles. In seeing them, he blessed them. He blessed them in their hardships, sorrows, best efforts, and crushing failures. The purpose of his blessing was to help them keep going. *Keep going*, he, in essence, said to them. Keep working for what you know is right. You may not see the fruits of your labors now, but I see them, and I see you. You are blessed.

If Jesus were to walk into this church today, I think he'd say much the same thing. Before standing before us to teach, he'd stop at each pew, look at every one of us directly and speak a word of blessing. Blessed are you, and you, and you, and you, and you. You are blessed in your worries, your doubts, and in your grief. You are blessed in your joy, creativity, and compassion. Keep going. Don't' worry about the big leaps. Concentrate on putting one foot in front of the other, being faithful in the little things, as those whom you honor today did in their lifetimes. Let my strength and my courage flow through you. It doesn't belong to you, but it is there for you, and through you, for others.

This closing prayer comes from the *Book of Common Prayers*, page 308.

> *Heavenly Father, we thank you that by water and the Holy Spirit you have bestowed upon us your servants the forgiveness of sin, and have raised us to the new life of grace. Sustain us, O Lord, in your Holy Spirit. Give us an inquiring and discerning heart, the courage to will and to persevere, a spirit to know and to love you, and the gift of joy and wonder in all your works. Amen.*

---

1. Taylor Branch, *Parting the Waters: America in the King Years, 1954-63* (New York: Simon & Schuster, 1988), p. 145.

2. Peter Gomes, "Our Turmoil, Inner Strength," in *Strength for the Journey* (San Francisco: HarperSanFrancisco, 2003), pp. 143, 147.

3. Desmond Tutu, *God Has a Dream: A Vision for Our Time* (New York: Doubleday, 2004), pp. 71-72.

LaVergne, TN USA
27 January 2010
171197LV00010B/61/P